Poems

Camilla Toulmin

BIBLIOBAZAAR

POEMS

BY

CAMILLA TOULMIN.

———◆———

LONDON:

Wᴹ· S. ORR & CO., PATERNOSTER ROW.

MDCCCXLVI.

CONTENTS.

* The Author has to acknowledge the courtesy of Mr. How, by whose
permission she reprints in this volume "The Song of the Trees,"
"The Hand," and "Stanzas," from her illustrated work "Lays and
Legends Illustrative of English Life." She is also indebted to
the kindness of Messrs. W. & R. Chambers, and other Publishers, for
permission to include a few Poems which have appeared at different
times in their periodicals.

POEMS.

THE REAL AND THE IDEAL.

One of Earth, and one of Heaven,
    They are strangely knit for aye ;
Harder are they to be riven
    Than Man's spirit from the clay.
Twin-born as the human birth,
    Yet more strongly intertwin'd ;
Each, believe, is little worth
    That the other doth not bind.

Start not, Dreamer ! at the thought,
    Jove's Olympus touch'd the ground ;
And the Rose, with odour fraught,
    Wins it from the soil around.
"But in Poetry and Art,
    And within the subtle brain,
The IDEAL dwells apart,
    There in majesty to reign ;"

Cries he with a lip upcurl'd,
 And he asks with scornful air,
" ' The statue that enchants the world !'
 Think'st thou Woman is as fair ?"

It may be—or it may not ;
 But at least ye this will own,
Surely it has been your lot
 Separate beauties to have known ?
Here a lip, and there a finger,
 Now a brow, or swan-like throat,
That within the mem'ry linger,
 And like fairy visions float.
This then is the bright IDEAL
 Which—oh, never lose the clue,
While it borrows from the REAL,
 Is itself for ever TRUE !

Cold unto the Poet's heart,
 Words—that do imprison Thought ;
Bars—that show us but a part
 Of the glory he has caught.
Yet he knows that human feeling
 Is the one exhaustless mine,
Though the gold of his revealing,
 Worldling ! never can be thine.
Nature in her fairest mood,
 Or her sternest, still is REAL ;
Nature, *then*, by Poet woo'd,
 Leads him to the true IDEAL.

Can He think a lofty deed,
　Which has not been acted o'er ?
Oh ! a human heart to read,
　Is, of all, the deepest lore.
And the Real, Real World
　Is, since first was Poet here,
In the bright IDEAL furl'd,
　As the Earth in atmosphere.
'Tis the air the Spirit breathes,
　If I read the Thing aright,
Which all radiant thought enwreathes,
　Shedding round us Spirit-Light.

ASTROLOGY AND ALCHEMY.

"There are more things in heaven and earth, Horatio,
Than are dreamt of in your philosophy."—SHAKSPEARE.

SPEAK gently of those two wild dreams, nor curl the lip
    with scorn,
That ever, wearing human shape, such dreaming fools
    were born,
As they whose gorgeous errors shook the steadfast
    thrones of kings,
And shadow'd long the mental world with their out-
    spreading wings.
It was an Age of Darkness—yea, the mighty Mind of
    Man
Was struggling 'mid the brambles, which its pathway
    overran;
And feebly shone the star of Truth, which rises as we
    gaze,
Until at last we fain must hope 'twill shed meridian
    blaze:
But only near the horizon it glimmer'd to the view
Of the earnest ones of olden time—the seekers of the
    True!

Speak gently of those parents old, who, dying at the
    birth,
Brought forth their marvellous offspring, to shed upon
    the earth
The truth-enkindled, living light, which never shall be
    lost.
ASTRONOMY and CHEMISTRY !—oh, where can Science
    boast
Such peerless daughters as the two that time hath won
    at last
From travail of the teeming mind, through darksome
    ages past ?
It was a dazzling meteor, that well might lead astray
The bounding heart, which fain would soar above its
    home of clay,
To think the whirling Stars, that watch with their un-
    slumb'ring eyes,
Had power unseen to guide the reins of human destinies.
Oh ! surely 'twas no grovelling soul that first the
    thought did own,
Which link'd his Being to the Stars, upon their purple
    throne,
And mounting on the pinions strong, which only Faith
    can spread,
Disdain'd sometimes the rugged path that Reason loves
    to tread ;
And yet, methinks, with wounded wing, Faith often in
    the race
Did turn where Reasons' finger shew'd anon a resting-
    place.

It might be such indeed were few, and yet the daughter
    fair,
ASTRONOMY, that mounts the path, and doth its steepness
    dare,
Reveals the things and thoughts ,that ask of man more
    ample mind
Than in her old dead parent's dream were ever found
    entwined.

But see, the yet more duteous Child advances proudly now,
To twine a laurel-wreath around her Ancient Parent's brow,
And tell it was no baseless hope, by knaves and fools
    begot,
To merit but the passing sneer, or dull oblivion's lot,
Which lured the gray-beards on to strive, though terrors
    round them furl'd,
To form of meaner elements the Thing that rules the
    world !
The soulless—bless'd—accursèd Gold, which in life's
    tangled web •
Must weave its strange controlling thread till life itself
    shall ebb.
But CHEMISTRY, that boldly speaks in Wisdom's garb
    array'd,
And wrests from Nature secrets hid since first the world
    was made,
Which can detect the subtle part the radiant diamond
    hath,
And moves with steady, rapid march, in her extending
    path

Proclaims—so spake the great high priest* who trod
    behind the veil

Of her pure temple—that the thing at which the
    thoughtless rail

May prove among her triumphs mean, in those ad-
    vancing years,

Whose herald-shadow now, methinks, upon the earth
    appears :

A triumph mean, if not in vain, that cherish'd dream of
    old—

Compared with knowledge, that outweighs the earth's
    whole store of gold.

1843.

---

* Sir H. Davy, in one of his lectures, asserts not only the possibility
of the transmutation of metals, but the probability that such a discovery
will be made. He adds, however, " it would of course be useless."

TO THE BRAVE HEARTS!

"They are the silent griefs which cut the heart-strings."—FORD.

To the Brave Hearts!   Not theirs who rush
    To lead the furious Van,
When rising passions wildly crush
    Fear from the heart of Man;
When Nations look as Umpires on,
And Honour must be lost or won!

To the Brave Hearts!   No senate throng,
    Upheld by iron will;
Whose constancy in right or wrong
    Belongs to Action still;
While party-friends do cheer them on,
And Honour must be lost or won!

Drink to the Hearts which do not break,
    But suffer, and are true!
Not of a radiant beauty speak,
    But cheeks of pallid hue.
To mortal eyes their crowns are dim;
But fill the goblet to the brim!

To Genius, doomed with drooping wing
  To toil a sad life through,
Yet keeps itself a holy thing,
  With holy work to do.
To them who ne'er such birthright sold—
Abused God's gift—for tempting gold!

To Woman, in her common course,
  (True heroine's destiny,)
Who finds endurance still the source
  Of all her bravery.
Than warriors' courage more divine;
So pour to Hers the sparkling wine!

To them who racked by mortal pain,
  Yet do not lose their trust;
Where Mind doth o'er the body reign,
  Till this resolves to dust.
To Hearts that suffer, and are true,
Be minstrels' praise, and honour due!

AN INVOCATION.

Rise, Nations, from your trance of woe and wrong!
  Cast off the burden that oppresses still,
Crush the fell monster that hath ruled so long,
  And quench the fire that only kindles ill;
War! whose foul throne, incarnadined, is built
Of quivering clay; erected but by guilt;
Cemented but with blood and tears.   Recall
  The tinsel trappings that are round it cast,
  And let the hideous show stand forth at last,
Reveal'd a moment, ere it crumbling fall
Into the grave of bygone things; and yield
The garner'd trophies of each crimson'd field;
Bring the gay banners that have floated high,
  Tear down the laurels from the conqueror's brow,
And let us light, beneath the calm blue sky,
  Their funeral pile, and lay such relics low;
And the bright flame shall purify the earth,
Fit for true glory's advent, and its birth!

They who the latest win, are victors; so
  The wise and merciful shall rule at last.
Arise, ye Nations, from your dream, for, lo!
  The shadow of the coming change is cast

Upon the earth, the substance is so near.
Arise, and listen, Nations!—do ye hear
The full deep murmur of the gathering throng ?
Upon their breath Opinion floats along—
Opinion, which is Power. And this doth strain,
And rust, and loosen the accursèd chain
(Forged by foul custom of all loathsome ties,
But gilded o'er with vainest sophistries);
And it will rot and rot, till there shall be
One vigorous bound, and Man at last be free !

And in the future years which onward roll,
Earth's happier children shall, with pitying soul,
List to the stories of a bygone age,
Or turn with awe th' historian's gory page.
And they, perchance, will meet beneath its slime
Calm deeds, high thoughts, unreck'd of at the time,
Like jewels by a blind man found, and flung,
By chance, a heap of meaner things among;
Then will true heroes be the ones selected,
And their lives' lustre be at last detected;
Whose silent influence, with starry ray,
Proved the pure heralds of approaching day.
For these, and such as these, shall be entwined
    Laurels unfading as unstain'd; and they
Shall be remember'd, and their deeds enshrined
    In grateful loving hearts, when pass'd away,
Or buried deep, with half-forgotten things,
Beneath the dust Time scatters from his wings,

The warrior's fame shall rest.   And Verse shall tell,
And Music lend her rich and wondrous spell,
To hymn the greater triumphs; blushing both,
As if these twins divine indeed were loth
To recollect how they, in darker hour,
Misused the sceptre of their magic power.
But Harmony and Poesy's rare gift,
Alike their strains to noblest themes shall lift,
No more to lure in falsehood's subtle guise,
Or dull the wail of human agonies;
But prove themselves, what they should ever be,
Earth's revelations of divinity!

1841.

SPRING IS COMING!

——•——

Spring is coming! joyous spring!
See, the messengers that bring
Tidings, ev'ry heart to cheer,
That her advent bright is here;
See, the many-colour'd train,
Peeping up o'er glade and plain—
Crocuses, and snow drops white,
Struggle into sunny light,
And the violet of blue,
And the valley's lily too.
I could dream their fairy bells
Ring a merry chime that tells
Spring is coming!—and when they
Faint, and fade, and fall away,
'Tis, that long by winter nurst,
Their full hearts with joy have burst,
At the tidings that they bring,
" Spring is coming! welcome spring!"
Children we of northern skies,
Most her loveliness do prize—
Most, with longing hearts, we yearn
For her swift and sure return;
We who know the sullen gloom,
When the earth is Nature's tomb;

Well may we with heart and voice,
At the sweet spring-time rejoice!

Dwellers in more genial climes,
Not for you these passing rhymes;
Ye can never understand
The contrasts of our northern land.
Ye are not so great and wise,
Ye have lowlier destinies
Than the children of a zone
Where the wintry blasts are known.
But gaunt famine doth not stride
By the proud and wealthy's side;
There ye see not little feet
Press upon the frozen street,
While the infant's tearful eye
Tells its tale of misery.
When in curtain'd, lighted hall,
What to such that snow-flakes fall?
When beside the blazing log,
What to them is frost or fog?
When on down their limbs they stretch
Think they of the homeless wretch?
To *the poor* it is that spring
Doth her richest treasures bring;
And methinks that I can hear
Countless voices, far and near,
Joining in a grateful strain,
" Spring is come at last again!"

March 4, 1842.

SONG OF A FLOWER SPIRIT.

When first the sunbeams linger
  To chase dark winter's gloom,
My Queen commands I bring her,
  A wreath of perfect bloom.
Beneath the earth I hide me,
  And nestle near each root,
And watch whate'er betide me,
  The tender seedlings shoot.
But if cold winds are blowing,
  My ready wings I spread,
To shield the stems from knowing
  The danger they would dread.

Oh, joy, when Zephyr's breathing
  Bids every leaf unfurl,
My tiny form enwreathing
  Within some palest curl !
And there I whisper boldly,
  " Obey the sweet decree,
Take not the kisses coldly
  The warm sun showers on thee! "

And so to all I wander—
  A message take to each ;
Do mortals pause and ponder
  The Truths that flowers teach ?

My Queen instructs the fairies,
  With the wreath upon her brow ;
And she sighs to think how rare is
  The bliss that earth should know.
But I 've heard her tell them often,
  That the God who made the Flowers,
Meant human hearts to soften,
  Through many joyous hours :
That o'er valley, plain, and mountain
  The Type of Joy upsprings,
That 'tis only Error's fountain
  Which can soil their spirit's wings !

NIGHT.

It was an idle, dreamy hour,
O'er which the fairy Mab had power,
    By whose arch will
Dark " spirits from the vasty deep,"
And such as in the flowerets sleep,
Or in the air, or on the earth—
All Sprites that owe to Fancy birth,
    Obey her still.
And so athwart a mortal brain
Strange pictures pass,—a motley train.
Methought, a moment, that she yielded
   Her magic sceptre to my reach,
And as the potent wand I wielded,
   A sprite replied with human speech.
It was the Spirit of the gorgeous Night!
The grand, the holy, thought-inspiring Night!
I heard, but not beheld—the sprite was hid
   By the thick shadow of an ebon cloud;
Yet when mine eyes from 'neath each drooping lid
   Would pierce the depths of ether, as aloud
      I him besought with fairy spell,
      That he his mysteries would tell,
      I felt such spirits pure must dwell

c

Throughout the Universe !   Oh, surely they
    Are kindred to the spirit half of man ;
And this is why they joyfully obey
    The spirit's invocations :—and thus ran
In broken and disjointed strain, perforce,
The mystic questioning of our wild discourse.

" Tell me, Spirits of the Night,
    Wherefore holy Night was made,
With its golden eyes of light,
    Piercing through the depths of shade ?

" For another boon I sue,
    Tell me, Spirits of the Night,
What for ever do ye view
    With your thousand eyes of light ?"

" Gather from more lowly things,
    Why was sent the gorgeous Night ;
Then beneath her sable wings,
    We will shed a spirit light ;
Whether good or ill betide
We will show what Night doth hide !"

" Once again the bond renew :
    Tell me, Spirits of the Night !
What for ever do ye view
    With your thousand eyes of light ?"

" Mount, mortal, on the undulating ray
Of yon bright star;—awhile the garish day
Has veil'd not quench'd its lustre—for the stars
Need not to rest upon their golden cars,
They pierce the vast unmeasured ether, though
The day's white hood doth hide them, till below
The western wave it folds : less wearied than
The feeble, fragile worm, mankind calls Man,
The stars unresting shine. Mount, mortal, now,
Mount on the bending ray, and it shall show
What thou dost seek.—Just as it shines, it shone
O'er the red field of glorious Marathon ;
And softly beam'd with ray as pure and bright
Upon Egyptia's wakeful shepherd's sight,
Startling to life the rare and *goodly* tree
Of Knowledge—SCIENCE that should ever be
Majestic spouse of radiant POESY !"

It is a gorgeous hall, where fair forms meet,
And to the swell of music, tiny feet
Move in the graceful measure. Hangings rare
Fall as a bulwark 'gainst the chilly air,
And yet the star-beam finds a chink, I ween,
And gleams upon the revels' youthful queen.
Youthful she is, and beautiful, men say ;
But Spirits, floating on the starry ray,
See spirit beauty, and this dulls the sense
To meaner, earthy loveliness ; and hence
She seems less lovely than the soulless gems

That shine like stars upon her night-black hair,
Or the pure flowers—that gather'd from their stems,
   Rear'd but for this with wondrous art and care,
To fade and wither on her Parian breast,
And pine in dying for a holier rest !
Her lord stands near her !   On his wrinkled brow,
Unmelting drifts of many winters' snow
Proclaim that he has reached at least the span
The Psalmist's lesson measures out to man.
From his dull eye no spirit lustre shines ;
No lofty word with noble deed combines
A woman's pure and priceless heart to win.
The gold his coffers clasp seems 'neath his skin
To flow in molten tide.   'Tis an old tale,
At which the careless world by fits doth rail,
And yet the actors honour ; she hath sold
Herself for power incarnate, magic gold !
Before Earth's altars she is called a wife,
And so—Earth honours her unhallowed life !

" Enough," methought I heard the Spirit say ;
" Mount, mortal, now upon a feebler ray."
It is the youngest Pleiad that looks down
Upon the world which cost her brighter crown.
Too trite the story is for modern verse,
   Though full of beauty is that poet's dream,
Thought kindling, as it does her woes rehearse,
   And tell the history of her fainter beam ;
Showing a moral beautiful and true,
Though thither led by fancy's silken clue.

Faintly it shines as in a human eye
Long years of grief will shroud its brilliancy ;
But mid the sparkling host I fain could think,
  With pitying heart the Pleiad's ray doth come
As if to earth still bound with one fond link
  The cold clear sky were not her proper home !
And mounting on the ray, and mingling there,
The spirit-power awhile again I share ;
And so look down upon the Ocean deep,
That doth so well its own dread secrets keep.
Oh ! how the labouring waves upheave and roll,
As if they sought to reach some far off goal ;
Obedient to their queen, whose sure behest
Forbids the ocean-tides one hour of rest.
She beckons from her starry court !   The sea,
In calm, or storm, obeys her high decree.
Is there not likeness here of human life ?
Each wave a soul, in calm, or storm, or strife,
Whose little span of time rolls quickly by
Upon the bosom of eternity !
Whether decreed to catch each gorgeous ray
  Down flung upon it by the lavish sun,
  And gladden, when its own bright course is run,
The thirsty golden sand with silver spray ;
  Or when the winds, from out great Ocean's cave
Summon the sleeping spirits of the storm,
  To ride upon each madly foaming wave,
And war with man, and all that man can form !
But now beneath the deep blue spangled arch
A stately ship moves on with graceful march :

How regally she treads!—her gilded prow
Stoops to the coming wave, as queens might bow
To faithful vassals kneeling at their feet.
And whither is she bound?—'Twere surely meet
So fair a thing should bask 'neath sunny skies,
And compass only happy destinies.
Do merry hearts wile early night away
With tale, or jest, or minstrel's softer lay?
Or lull'd by ocean, in their oak-bound home
Dream of the gorgeous lands to which they roam?
Or doth some care-worn wanderer vigils keep
Sick with home yearnings, which have banished sleep?
Or bears she ingots of the yellow ore,
And merchant's wealth, of every varied store?
She is a stately bark, and hath a fairy name,
                              Which may she claim?
Neither.   It is a CONVICT SHIP, that like a queen
Treads the deep waters with majestic mien!
Oh! that there were some mighty spirit spell
By which the coldly good one hour could tell
The cables which dread Circumstance can weave,
    To strain from right the feeble heart of man!
Yet were it so, soft Pity's tears would leave
    No strength for justice, and its needful plan.
Methinks 'tis easy for us, happier born,
With kindling eye, and lip that curls with scorn,
To marvel that the boundary lines we own
(Which rise from seed that near our path was sown,)
Should not hedge round from Error's yawning grave,
And wretched Ignorance from misery save.

NIGHT.

Oh, CIRCUMSTANCE,—a Janus front is thine!
Oh, IGNORANCE! for whom no beacons shine!
Thou always dost some dangerous precinct haunt,
And leap to Crime, when sharply spurred by Want!

Yes, 'tis a crew, in vice and misery steeped,
Whose sins, like coals on feeble embers heaped,
Dull'd, for long years, the ever quenchless flame
   Of conscience ; which upspringing fiercely now,
Burns in—a deeper brand, than that of shame. .
   Some broken spirits meekly learn to bow ;
Some, in the anguish of their wild despair,
Feel speechless woe " more great than they can bear."
But 'mid that band rejected, and outcast,
Is one on whom the vengeful law has passed
An *unjust sentence !* (for such things must be—
Frailty's the badge of all humanity.)
He sleeps, and soundly ;—while the searching beam
Kindles a halo, o'er his brow to gleam.
He sleeps, and soundly ; though the throng around
Break the night's stillness, with a wailing sound ;
Made up of sobs, and sighs, and words of gloom,
Anon, deep curses at their self-wrought doom.
But though for him life's sunshine all is o'er,
And earth's pure joys for him shall spring no more,
With even pulse, he lays him down to rest,
For conscience smiles, and lulls the aching breast.
It is remorse that lends to human grief
The poison sting that never finds relief.
Perchance kind Hope *may* paint with fairy hue

In coming days the triumph of the True.
Meanwhile, with brow serenest of them all,
The guiltless man, though bound with guilt's sharp thrall,
Moves in his dark and narrow path, and still
Can find a glory through the mists of ill.
And now he understands King David's choice,
Besought of Heaven with a humble voice,—
The choice, to be chastised of God alone ;
And so his heart dictates " THY will be done ! "

" Enough," the Spirit sighed, " enough is shown :
Choose now a star that gems the Boreal Crown."
And, like a feather drifted by the wind,
My soul obeyed the spell the Spirit twined !
There is a chamber rude—a casement high,
And one poor watcher of the starry sky.
His day's too needful toil at length is past,
When the bowed heart with joy upsprings at last.
Lofty the brow the night winds softly fan,
But the supporting hand is weak and wan ;
(And, oh ! methinks the observing eye may trace
Expression here, not art, nor will, can chase.)
THE MAN BEFORE HIS AGE !—alone—apart
From the dull throng communes with his own heart !
'Tis well !—For every faculty has bent
To one great purpose, and one sole intent.
Crushed by the iron heel of Poverty,
Not his to form affection's holiest tie ;
No loving wife, or prattling child is near,
The care-worn student's hour of rest to cheer.

And through all ages such the minds who still
" Our spirits rule," and Fame's bright records fill,
More often lone than with the shield
From half life's ills a *happy* home can yield.
More often lone :—for in the wheel of life
How oft has Genius drawn but woe and strife !
Or is it that each faculty and sense
To mate the intellect is deep—intense—
So that for them, there ever sparkles up,
Either the nectar or the poison cup ?
I know but this, that as the marble rock
Is fretted by the river's feeble shock,
Although an earthquake threw it up unrent,
When all the elements of power were blent ;
So the proud heart of Genius, day by day,
Girt by domestic misery, wears away.
Thus—for the thankless world—perchance 'tis best,
No human ties find anchor in His breast.
He had a glorious dream in days of yore,
But now a score of years are passed—and more ;
Love's flowers are dead, or faded all,
Though kept like relics beneath memory's pall.
And ever since the hour when the decree
Of that gaunt despot, iron Poverty,
Went forth to quench Hope's bright and cheering light,
And blast Love's flowers, which bloomed beneath his sight;
The expanding mind, braced by the shocks of fate,
Stands forth the mightier, and more concentrate.
THE MAN BEFORE HIS AGE—THE PIONEER !
Who cries " Eureka," and the herd but jeer;

And yet the pathway that he leaves behind,
The broad foot-marks which they that follow find,
Lead—if to future years we quickly leap,
To the rich harvest meaner minds shall reap.
Perchance in earlier days a meteor flame
Lured him to dream of winning earthly fame.
But this is over—and no visions now
Image the laurel round his fading brow;
They only whisper, that a future age
Of wiser men shall venerate his page.
So, as the bright beam from the starry crown
　　Meets the raised orbs which Genius' fire illumes,
Kissing the cheek whence health's clear hue is flown,
　　And the bent frame, that slow decay consumes,
Unto his heart it seems a type on high
Beyond the pale of poor mortality.
Methinks to many a world-wearied mind,
That Northern Crown, so clear, so well defined
Hath whispered the soul's language—which must be
Those deathless Truths, whose Truth is Poetry!
(For it doth seem no other word expresses
The dim revealings which the soul confesses.)
It tells of something dearer to such hearts
Than earthly fame, or earthly crown imparts.
This is the spirit-essence which is found
In pure religion, and is shed around
The soul of Genius, where it doth distil,
And lowlier minds with borrowed glory fill.
He asks no guerdon now from feeble man,
But feels his soul a part of the Almighty Plan!

Just as a vapour doth a mirror dim,
   Sudden, confused, a cloud came o'er my sight ;
No longer might I pause to gaze on him
   Whose soul I read beneath the Star-Crown light.
Where chained Andromeda to fancy's ears
Wails out her heart with piteous moans and tears,
Mine eye obedient turned—thence to behold
Her stars shed down a stream of rippling gold ;
For are not starlight's intermittent rays
Like sun-kissed waters when the west wind plays?
And these look down where Poverty's strong hand
Binds human hearts with more than iron band—
Yea, with the pressure of more biting pain
Than e'er was known from captive's galling chain.
Behold a Poor House of the Modern School,
The trial test of Atheistic rule !
Bravely it works ! the wheels keep measured time
To Mammon's chuckle for their guiding chime !
While a deep bass of swelling sobs and groans
   Floats its sad music to a pitying God ;
More feebly heard by Man, half deaf to tones
   Wrung from the wretched by Oppression's rod.
Yet as by use each sense grows quick and clear,
So we but listen we distinctly hear,
And find a prayer in every piercing cry,
Appeal from Man to Man in every heart-wrung sigh.

We know there is a tale, old, worn-out, trite—
Dang'rous, because of truth it has its mite
(For Satan, in his hour of vengeful gloom,

Weaves with waste shreds from Truth's celestial loom)—
Men, moving through the world devoid of heart,
And so brain-weakened to perform their part,
Perceive the earth produces food enough,
Apparel too, and every proper stuff,
So all mankind would toil with strength and skill,
And use the cunning hand with cunning will.
" None need to beg, there 's work for all ! " they cry ;
And so—the question settled—pass it by !
And you, proud, prosperous, energetic man,
Who square all rules to this cold, selfish plan—
Who cannot understand a weaker mind
Grows feebler still with misery intertwined
(The very blast our northern frames to brace,
Would quench the life of India's feebler race),
Is it your merit that you were not born.
A being such as them you coldly scorn ?
Of race corrupt, tried, tempted, fallen too—
The Angels pity, though your scorn pursue—
While every CIRCUMSTANCE of Life's young day
Conspired to check the right or lure astray ?
Pray, have you known what 'tis to starving lie,
And fuel want ? or, only not to die,
Earning what farmers can afford to give,
The shillings few which let the labourer—live ?
If so, vouchsafe the secret to explain,
    How such may save 'gainst sickness' deadly hour,
Or the—for them too many—years of pain
    When Age has robbed the wearied limbs of power ?
No reverence for the Patriarchal Poor

Has Mammon's sons ; and yet of this be sure,
High hearts to them of all most truly tender,
Instinctive homage Youth to Age should render.
The tillers of the fruitful teeming earth,
With used up sinews, now so little worth !
Oh, that machines they might become, and so
Escape this cruel heritage of woe !
Not need the coarse, begrudged, and scanty meal,
And cease at once to recollect or feel,
Or pine for kindreds' now forbid caress,
Or ought that God vouchsafed mankind to bless !
Oh England, not the laurels that you wear
Can hide this brand upon your forehead fair !
A brand that grows the deeper day by day.
Oh ! cease the Wrong, and let it wear away !

The Stars look down on every human thing—
Do they a message of deliverance bring ?
" Yea," and methought a joyous spirit broke
A moment's silence, and the echoes woke
As if to claim a chorus for his strain—
Prophetic of Earth's new and happier reign.

God is a Spirit—by Spirit HE works—
   By the Mighty Mind of Man !
Look at it right—there grandeur lurks
   Unfolding HIS righteous Plan.
Like tapestry-workers, we see but a part
   Of the beautiful fabric we weave ;
Yet every earth-child with a thoughtful heart

On the earth his work must leave.
These have to rectify all the mistakes
  Of the erring who wrought before;
By the dawn which athwart the horizon breaks
  May we see—not to err any more!

What the Past Ages the Earth has rolled!
  After all, 'tis a Baby World;
For the Future rests with its days untold
  In Eternity's womb yet furl'd!
In the swathing-clothes of error and fear
  Man has been cramped, we know;
But the vigorous limbs plunge there and here,
  They do their bonds outgrow.
From within—from within the strength must rise,
  Which shall shatter them all at length;
Adored be HIM who Ever Wise
  Wills Truth alone be Strength!
Yea, though for ages battling long,
  Weaving Its martyr's crowns—
Or humbly hid in minstrel's song,
  Or daring monarchs' frowns;
Clasped in some long-neglected tome,
  Yet writ upon the sky—
And uncorrupt whatever come
  To dim its radiancy!

The Stars from their thrones on high look down
  With a trembling fear and hope,
To mark how the Human Mind has grown,

And to watch its farther scope.
And they pierce to the homes of the great and good,
    Where the subtle brain is working,
And they see where True Wisdom loves to brood,
    There Virtue is near her lurking—
Hidden sometimes, like flowers by weeds;
    But, like Truth, She cannot die,
And wherever she sojourns she casteth seeds
    That shall bloom eternally.
And they read the signs of the thoughtful Now,
    And not the least they find
Are that Science and Peace are on its brow,
    And that Woman 's a cultured mind;
And they see that Man's mighty Soul is bent
    On a better order of things,
And they know It is God's own instrument
    With which all change HE brings !

THE HAND.

WHAT is it fashioned wondrously, that, twin born with
the Brain,

Marks Man from every meaner thing that bounds across
the plain,

Or gambols in the mighty deep, or floats in summer
air,

What is the help meet for the Mind, no lesser life may
share ?

It is the Hand, the Human Hand, interpreter of Will ;

Was ever servant yet so great, and so obedient still ?

Of all Creation's mysteries with which the world is rife,

IT seems a marvel to my soul but second unto Life !

How weak a thing of flesh it is, yet think what IT has
done !

And ask from poor Idolators why it no worship won ?

How could the lordly forest trees first bow their heads
to Man,

When with their ruined limbs he delved where veins of
metal ran ?

Ho ! ho ! 'tis found, and his to know the secrets of the
forge ;

And henceforth Earth, at his behest, her riches must
disgorge.

And now the Hand has servants fit, IT guides as it is
    schooled,
To keep entire the perfect chain by which the world is
    ruled.
For when the molten iron flowed into the first rough
    mould,
The heritage of cunning craft was to the Right Hand
    sold ;
And IT hath been a careful lord, improving every right,
Until the Mind is overawed by thinking of its might.
How slender, and how fair a thing, is woman's soft white
    hand !
Yet Saragoza's Maid could seize the cannon's ready
    brand ;
And martyr'd Joan—(but not of War or carnage would I
    tell,
Unless the time were ripe and mine the deep-toned
    honoured shell
With chords to be the requiem of the gory monarch
    dread,
Whose laurels still, though steeped in tears, conceal his
    leprous head !)
The harp is roused by fingers fair, where clinging jewels
    glow
With light upon the awakening hand like sunbeams upon
    snow ;
Entrancèd Music's soul returns once more to earth
    again—
A vassal to the Hand that wills a gay or pensive strain.

Yet think—that Hand which never yet knew weariness
    or soil,
Whose fairness neither summer's sun nor winter's cold
    must spoil,
Which doth not know a harsher rule than leisure's chosen
    toil,
Is after all but fashioned like the trembling, clammy
    thing
With which the faded sempstress pale, in youth's yet
    early spring,
Digs her own grave, with needle small, through Nature's
    drowsy night.
Oh! when will Fortune, Justice, too, unbind their eyes
    to light!
How is it Fashion's proud array, thus wove on Death's
    own loom,
Ne'er changes by a demon spell to trappings of the
    tomb?

The Painter bodies forth ideas, which on the canvas live—
The Sculptor bids the shapeless stone a form of beauty
    give—
Wise Egypt's giant pyramids by human hands were
    piled,
To wrestle still with conquering Time, though centuries
    have smiled,
With gentle touch to think how they sweep Man from
    where he stands,
Yet linger o'er the records of his wonder-working hands!

It is a thought to lift the soul beyond its prison-home,
To ponder o'er such things as these beneath the fretted
dome
Of Gothic fane, where erst have swept the serge-clad
Monkish train,
Who sought to win their paradise by self-inflicted pain ;
Who never knew the worship true, that life's pure joys
impart.
Yet what a world and history is every human heart !
Alas! material monuments too oft, like Babel's tower,
But tell of human littleness, and not of human power !
More subtle, less self-evident, than marvels such as these,
Those spirit deeds that leave behind but dream-like
legacies,
Nothing that sense can see or touch, but much that
Thought can keep.
As when the stately ship is taught its pathway o'er the
deep
By one right hand that guides the helm, beneath the
watchful crowd
Of ever silent stars, that pierce through Nature's
nightly shroud.
But Thought is lost in mazy dreams of all the wondrous
band,
Of Things and Deeds that owe their birth unto the
Human Hand."

SONG OF THE LOST PLEIAD.

SHINE on, proud Sisters!—gem the sky,
But mock not ye my destiny!
Human I know my heart has grown,
But never for a shining Crown
Would I its human lore unlearn,
And to my radiance lost return.
Ye pity me my lowly choice,
But hear the Starry Bride rejoice!
  Sisters, believe my Crown is not
  A forfeit high for Love's sweet lot!

Strange, human love demands, they say,
The sacrifices mortals pay;
Yet wealth before its altars flung,
Or for a trophy, proudly hung,
Within its temple; fortune, fame,
And myriad hopes the heart could name,
Grow valueless, until they seem
Poor as the mem'ry of a dream!
  Sisters, my forfeit Crown is not
  Too high a price for Love's sweet lot!

Strange human love !   None ever thinks,
While the elixir draught she drinks,
Too high the price ;—and so no stain
Of shame doth like a brand remain,
If round the heart, beneath Love's wings
Gather all holy thoughts and things—
Ambition's tinsel toys are not
A forfeit high for Love's sweet lot !
   Then grieve not for my lowly choice,
   But hear the Starry Bride rejoice !

BREAD.

Bread, Bread! Eat and be welcome friends;
  Crumbs if ye will to the fowls of the air;
Or for your faithful dog leave broken ends;
  Brutes, oh, believe me, are worthy man's care.
Eat and be nourished, or give and be blessed—
  Aught in the wide world but waste or pollute it;
Touch it as something revered and caressed;
  Scorn or indifference never can suit it!

Think how the Harvest's God ripened the Corn,
  Call ye the growth of each young blade to mind—
Think how the summer sun rose every morn—
  Think how the laden spears waved in the wind!
Think as they gleamed there, more burnished than gold,
  Were they not war weapons serried for fight?
Marshalled to strive against hunger and cold,
  Each with a star for dark misery's night!

Think ere ye fling it disdainfully down,
  Of the sweat on the labourer's deep-furrowed brow!
I tell you if ye have in idleness grown,
  If nought of your *doing* on earth ye can show,

No matter your station, no matter your name,
  To him bend the knee, with a bending heart too ;
For homage, methinks, is the least he should claim,
  Who does double duty for self and for you !

Double duty !—your pardon ; oh ! were it but so,
  Did really one half of mankind do their part,
How quickly would close up the world's gulf of woe,
  And joy heal the wounds of its care-stricken heart !
Then honour to all who with Head or with Hand,
  Work wisely and well, and inherit the Earth ;
And scorn for the ignoble do-nothing band,
  Who are but the locusts that prey upon worth !

Eat of it gratefully, eat and be filled ;
  Think of the gaunt ones who hunger for Bread !
Be 'mong the thoughtless your lessons instilled ;
  Let bright example its influence shed !
Touch it as something revered and caressed,
  Scorn or indifference never can suit it ;
Eat and be nourished, or give and be blessed,
  Aught in the wide world but waste or pollute it !

ON THE COMPLETION OF THE THAMES TUNNEL.

Joy to thee, brave Brunel !— thy task is done,
Th' immortal wreath of fame is nobly won !
Not thine the warrior's stain'd and tear-dew'd crown,
Thou hast a loftier and more pure renown.
Joy to thee, brave Brunel !—thou hast been tried
By the *world's ordeal*, and SUCCESS hath dried
The well-springs of Distrust, whose waters deep
Engulf such precious things—or coldly steep
The heart of genius, until warped aside,
Or piecemeal rotted, by that ebon tide,
Its might and majesty alike are past :
But thine, Brunel, was of too stern a cast ;
Though round thee long had flowed those turbid waves,
Bearing upon their crests the ready glaives
Of ignorance—the bitter taunt and jest
That Folly, in its mischievous unrest,
Seizes with vacant laugh, and blindly flings
At dazzling genius on her soaring wings.
And yet, methinks, Distrust's dark icy stream
Did to thy noble heart through long years seem

More fearful than old Father Thames that roll'd
In loud defiance o'er thee ; who, controll'd
By the strong spell of science, meekly now
Learns in obedience to thy will to flow !
Oh ! how much greater art thou, brave Brunel !
Than Persia's king, who, as old histories tell,
Came with his millions, and but strove in vain
With all his might one rebel wave to chain.
Was there a mind like thine in all his train ?
And do not at such thoughts quick mem'ries throng,
Worthy a nobler bard and loftier song,
To tell how dark those wild and barbarous ages,
When warriors' deeds fill'd up the historian's pages ?
Now doth at least a twilight dawn ; men pay
With fame's bright garlands, not alone who slay,
But them who save and serve.   Joy, brave Brunel !
The new " world's wonder " is achieved, and well
By its own self is thy great soul repaid ;
And yet wert thou *as great*, ere yet arrayed
With the world's halo, that success has cast
Around thee (for mankind *are* just at last) ;
Thou wert as great when this " world's wonder " dwelt
Yet unembodied in the mind that felt
Its power to do and dare.   Did it then rise
In grand perfection to thy spirit's eyes,
Conceived one moment and matured the next
(As Wisdom's goddess in the heathen text,
Sprung forth all armed from the Thunderer's brain) ?
Or was it link by link, the perfect chain
Of thy so wonderful design was wrought
In the mind's mazes of most tangled thought ?

Whiche'er, it matters not, for then, as now,
As great thou wert, the thoughtful feel and know:
When thou didst take a lesson from the worm *
The strange secureness of thy work to form,
And show the precept men are slow to learn—
Nought God has made is low enough to spurn;
That loftiest Science most acutely feels
How vast the lore great Nature's law reveals.
Thou wert *as great*—yea, *greatest* in those years
Of silent grief and watching, when dark fears,
Methinks, must oft have dimm'd, or hidden quite
The cheering rays of hope's exceeding light.
The seven years ! in which no workman's stroke
Those arches' mute forgetful echoes woke.
But hark ! they have a tongue again, and dwell
No more in " cold obstruction "—brave Brunel !
Unquench'd by the dull flood of those long years,
Thy spirit's fire more purely bright appears;
And like a chain electric, runs through all
The busy crew who gathered at thy call;
Teaching them well to understand they shared
The glory of all that which thou hadst dared.
And didst thou life to wood and iron yield,
When thou didst sway thy ever trusty " Shield? " †

---

* The idea upon which Sir I. Brunel founded his system of tunnel-
ing was suggested to him by watching the operations of the teredo, which
eats its way through the hardest wood, and has on this account been
called the *Calamitas navium.*

† " This mighty instrument—one in idea and object, but consisting
of twelve separate parts or divisions, each containing three cells, one
above the other—is thus used :—We will suppose that the work being

Joy to thee, great Brunel ! thy task is done,
The immortal wreath of fame is nobly won !
Her clarion sounds, and thy name is the note
That echoes catch, and round the world doth float;
And this is guerdon worthy even thee ;
Ambition's dream made rich reality.
But is there not a joy more deep—intense,
The triumph of thy work's own recompense ?
Doth not *this* give to nature's beauteous face
Some added charm or once unheeded grace ?

---

finished in its rear, an advance is desired, and that the divisions are in
their usual position, the alternate ones a little before the others. These
last have now to be moved.   The men in their cells put down the top
poling-board, one of those small defences with which the entire front of
the shield is covered, and immediately cut away the ground for about
six inches.   That done, the poling-board is replaced, and the one below
removed, and so on till the entire space in front of these divisions has
been excavated to the depth of six inches.   Each of the divisions is
now advanced by the application of two screws, one at its head and
one at its foot, which, resting against the finished brick-work, and
turned, impel it forward into the vacant space.   The other set of divi-
sions then advance.   As the miners are at work at one end of the cells,
so the bricklayers are no less actively employed at the other forming
the brick walls of the top, sides, and bottom, the superincumbent earth
of the top being still held up by the shield till the bricklayers have
finished.   This is but a rude description of an engine almost as remark-
able for its elaborate organisation as for its vast strength.   Beneath
those great iron ribs a kind of mechanical soul really seems to have
been created.   It has its shoes and its legs, and uses them, too, with
good effect.   It raises and depresses its head at pleasure ; it presents
invincible buttresses in its front to whatever danger may there threaten,
and, when the danger is past, again opens its breast for the further ad-
vances of the indefatigable host."—" *London ;*" *article,* " *The Thames
Tunnel.*"

Surely more bright each earthly thing appears
Than in the night of those long struggling years.
Joy to thee, brave Brunel!—I do not know
From the dull common crowd that thoughtful brow,
Where Mind hath fixed her glowing diadem;
Yet wilt thou not my lowly verse condemn,
Or spurn the homage I but feebly pay;
The heartfelt tribute of my humble lay !

LONDON, *June,* 1842.

THE DEATH OF THE PAUPER PEASANT. *

"Princes and lords may flourish, or may fade,
A breath can make them, as a breath has made ;
But a bold peasantry, their country's pride,
When once destroy'd, can never be supplied."—GOLDSMITH.

'NEATH the summer's sun, and the winter's snow,
   Through Youth and Manhood's time,
He won by the toil that furrow'd his brow
   Deep, in his early prime,
The homely food, and the garments rude,
   And shelter from wind and weather ;
Up—up with the sun, his work was begun
   Ere the birds sprung from the heather.
      Plough—sow—delve away,
       The harder the work, the less the pay ;
          Do we not know
          The world goes so ?

* See case reported in the *Times*, Dec. 1843.

But the shelter that kept out weather and winds
　Had the magical name of Home ;
A word that is dearer to English minds
　Than palace or lordly dome.
There were garments rude, and homely food,
　For a little loving band ;
And a wife was there, once young and fair,
　To clasp the horny hand,
And bless it—through God—that its strength could give,
Not store for old age—but the means to live !
　For the poor have hearts—and 'tis thought they know,
　A feeling of joy from one of woe.

Old Age—*he* hath pass'd by years the span
That the Psalmist, we know, "measured out to man,"
And Fortune, the blind, for him doth rehearse
The mournful and terrible Roman curse.
His children have grown greyheaded—and died,
Why doth he not lie in the grave beside ?
For England is bleak to the poor and old,
She knoweth no worth but the worth of gold;
She doth not attempt to understand
The noble labour of head or hand;
Her soul must be dead, if it never mounts
To a Heaven beyond "red-lined accounts !"

And the horny hand is feeble now,
　And the full bright eye is dim ;
And his scanty hairs are white as snow,
　And he totters in every limb.

Yet may it not be, that memory
Lives through the wreck of years ?
Does he call on Death, with that gasping breath,
  And the fast descending tears ?
                Oh ! the world is cold
                To the Poor and Old,
For he cannot work, and he doth not steal,
And only the poor for him can feel !

'Tis Poverty gaunt the shelter gives,
  And a homely couch spreads there ;
Though she can no more, and only lives
  Herself on the scantiest fare,
But she *hath* kind words, that wake the chords
  Of grateful tenderness !
Oh, spoils the least, of the wealthy's feast,
  Would soothe the hours' distress !
                But the Law says, " No,
                It must *not* be so ;
Away from the scene that mirrors Home—
Away, to the parish workhouse come !"

Life's sands are ebbing few and fast ;
Thank God, he hardly knows at last,
The meaning of the words they say !
" Up—up, Old Man ! come—come away,
Though cold and wet December's day ;"
But harsher than the melting sky
The hearts that turn him forth—to die.

A pauper dies—what matter where ?
Or how he lives, they little care.
Is Poverty so deep a crime,
Bears it the brand—the serpent's slime,
So plainly marked, that by its side
Seems fair the selfish heart of pride ?
That Idleness and Luxury
Are worthier held than Poverty ?
No !   Honour to the stalwart hand,
And honour to the labouring band !
And though the Pauper's winding sheet
Is all Old England now can mete
To him who till'd her fruitful soil,
Till Age forbade the hand to toil ;
Deep in the heart such things shall sink—
Deep in the hearts that feel and think,
Until OPINION'S mighty sway,
Shall wipe the Nation's stain away !

December, 1843.

LONDON BY MOONLIGHT.

THE midnight hour has pass'd away, and yet
The Queen of Night still holds her starry court ;
The tangled clouds sail swiftly by,—and now
She bathes the city in a flood of Light !
Far other than the proud and garish day,
Like Charity, her mild and gentle beams
Soften, or hide, each rude and broken line ;
Prisons and palaces !   And stately domes,
And hovels mean !

                         The dreaming poet loves
To muse 'mid shady groves, and by the side
Of clear and murmuring streams ; but, rather here
May Contemplation find its food and dwell
On man,—God's latest, and most wondrous work.
And thou, proud River ! I can scarcely heed
That on thy shores, where thou dost wander 'mid
The green and smiling fields,—the shepherd lays
His crook, and slumbers in the noon-day heat :
For, from the stream which flows like molten lead
Beneath the moonbeams, I behold a grove
Of masts against the starry sky.   The wealth,

E

The argosies of princely merchants here,
That to the ear of fancy whisper tales
Of far-off climes, and England's power and pride.
Yon stately vessel only waits the dawn
To raise aloft her snowy sails, that then
Shall bear her, "like a thing of life," away,
Though now she rests like a fond child upon
A doting mother's breast.   And all is still,
Save the soft ripple of the rising tide.
Thou gorgeous city of our pride and love!
But yonder Abbey wakens other thoughts—
The hearts of kings and statesmen, warriors, bards,
Lie there entomb'd—the Mighty of the Earth,
The dust for rolling centuries revered,
And they the honoured of a recent age :
He of the rude, untaught, unletter'd mind,
Innately great, beside the darling child
Of arts advanced, and years more wonderful !
In this alike the lesson which they teach,
That Death shall level all.   And yet, methinks,
It is a soul-inspiring thought to lure
The adventurous spirit on to noble deeds,
The thought, that all which ever did belong
To earth, perchance, shall rest beside the good
And great ; while faithful records shall enshrine
The subtler part within the grateful hearts
Of future unborn ages.

                                        Turn we now
To yon large gloomy pile—the abode of guilt

And wretchedness.   Yet Virtue stays to weep ;
For she is all too wise and pure to fear
That tears, e'en for the guilty, e'er can stain
One dazzling fold in which herself is wrapt.
Oh, Virtue stern and cold were liker far
A statue, than the warm and breathing form
Which mortals long to clasp !   Alas ! she knows
The tempter's power, which comes in equal strength,
Though vary'd guise, unto the silken couch
And pallet rude,—and, though she dares not touch
The scale of Justice, turns aside to weep !

Mark you the faint and glimmering light which falls
From yonder casement dim ?—is it the watch
Untiring love still keeps beside the bed
Of death or sickness ?—or doth there the young
Aspiring student seek to hive the store,
The golden priceless store, from wisdom's page ?—
Or doth an aching heart forbid the eye
To close ?   Imagination quickly weaves
A thousand unsubstantial webs,—and now
The Sleeping City, in its hush'd repose,
Looks like the phantom of its waking self !

There is a burst of revelry that breaks
Upon the solemn stillness of the hour ;
But near the boisterous crew which homeward wends
Gaunt Famine stalks, and holds the shrivell'd hand.
Ah, yes ! they turn, the homeless wretch relieve.—
I cannot hear her low and broken words ;

But they, the young and gay, are silent now,—
The chord of sympathy, by pity waked,
Has dull'd their selfish mirth!

                        But morning breaks
In all its glory.   See ! the silver moon
Has doff 'd her shining crown, and all the stars,
That made the sky a jewell'd mirror, melt
In the pale azure of the early dawn.
Man wakes again to joy, and peace, and hope,
Day-dreams, and bright reality,—to toil,
Or ease and luxury—alas ! as well
To pain and sin, to care and suffering !

    1838.

BIRTHDAY THOUGHTS.

ADDRESSED TO ————.

———•———

'Tis a Birthday ! You know whose :
One year added unto those
Which came round so very fast,
That we said, upon the last,
We would chronicle no more,
Till had passed another score !

Well ! the sky is just as blue
As it was in former years ;
Roses have the selfsame hue,
And each summer flower appears
Gracefully to raise its head,
While its fragrant wealth is shed,
As when rudely from their stem
We young children severed them,
To compose a plaything wreath.
Just the same the hawthorn's breath,
As when, in the studious hour,
It had a forbidden power ;
For, while stealing o'er our senses,
Thought was lured from present " tenses "

To the shady garden plot,
Or the fields where books were not.
There 's the old clock striking ten !
Is it study-hour again ?
Yea, but not from grammar book,
Or in school-room's prison'd nook
Read we, as we ponder thus,
Of the change that is in us !

Yonder oak tree—not a bit
Has it grown—I'm sure of it,
Since against its sturdy bark
Measured we our three feet height,
And indented there the mark,
Which, alas ! is vanish'd quite.
Tell me—wouldst thou, if we could,
Recall one hour of childhood's years ?
With its April smiles and tears,
With its trembling hopes and fears ;
These so little understood,
That a young child's woe or mirth,
Is the loneliest thing on earth !
For the Future castle-building,
With bright fancy's ready gilding,
May not be the wisest way
We can pass an hour to-day ;
But methinks 'twere quite as wise,
As to turn with longing eyes,
To the years that dropp'd so fast
In that grave we call the Past.

Earth grows richer every day
In the wealth that mind must sway.
So, though the sky be still as blue—
The summer clouds as fleecy too,—
The flowers as bright—the thrush's note
As richly to the ear doth float,
As when our tiny footsteps strayed
In garden trim, or emerald glade,
Let us with hearts contented own
That *we* the only change have known !

THE EARLY SETTLERS.

How strange a dream it seems to me,
  To me now grey and old,
To ponder over hours, since which
  Full fifty years have roll'd !
But busy memory opens yet
  Her thickly crowded page,
Whose characters I still can trace
  Undimm'd by time or age.

More vivid far those pictures be
  Than scenes more new and nigh,
For Youth's warm records, they are stamp'd
  With Memory's deepest dye.
Again I see that far-off land,
  And hear the City's din,
And her, the gentle fair-hair'd Girl,
  Again, in thought, I win !

Our heritage was Youth and Love,
  And Hope with fairy wand,
(Ah ! princes oft would change for these
  Their sceptre, gold, and land.)

But Time, which beauty makes or mars,
    Hath silver'd Her fair hair
And dimm'd her eye, yet still I read
    Affection's language there !

Where then primeval forests stood,
    The yellow corn now bends,
And with the nearer hum of bees,
    Yon mill's harsh music blends !
Our grandchild's children prattle round,
    While I muse o'er our lot,
Beneath the shadow of the tree
    I planted on this spot !

The giant hills, which only heard
    The wild bird's lonely shriek,
Now echo back, on every side,
    The language Britons speak !
There's something glorious in such thoughts
    Which banishes regret,
Howe'er it chance that Memory now
    Forbids me to forget !

And here these aged limbs shall rest
    When death's rude grasp shall come ;
The founder of a vigorous race
    Needs no mausoleum !
'Twill soothe that hour to know I leave
    A happy, prosperous band ;
My blessing rest upon the soil
    That is *their Fatherland !*

1839.

SONG OF THE WINTER BLAST.

FROM the frozen clime of my birth, afar,
    Is begun my fitful march ;
Where the golden car
Of the bright Pole Star
    Is the key of heaven's blue arch !
While for ever around its steadfast throne
Seem to whirl, one by one,
(As if they were vassals, who, meek and true,
Thus to their liege pay homage due,)
The orbs that move on, as they circled of old,
Led by the Bear and the Hunter bold,*
        Which as they bound
        Round and round,
        Measure the flight
        Of the long, long night,
        That reigns for the time,
        Which in softer clime
Maketh two seasons upon the earth.
But bright is the Dome 'neath which I have birth,

---

* The constellation Boötes; the fable of which is, that with his two dogs he is perpetually driving the Bear round the Pole.

Where the Boreal lights, like banners unfurl'd,
Shed their glory upon the Northern World ;
And the silver band of the galaxy,
Like a loosen'd girdle, spans the sky.
 From this Polar home,
 Where no man may roam,
 I burst through the cleft
 Of an ice-berg reft,
And my hitherward course began.
 Over pillars of ice and plains of snow,
 Prepared for my coming ages ago,
My chosen pathway ran.
 Till I leap'd with a bound
 Which echo'd around
 To Norway's rocky shore.
 Then with threat'ning roar,
 In my hurried race,
 I shook the spectre larch,
 Or with rough embrace,
 As I onward march,
 My caresses are known
 By the full deep moan
Which the pine-tree breathes to me ;
 Or in anger and strife
 I war with their life,
And uproot each lordly tree.

Now again on the shore, where the cataracts leap
From on high to the dark and fathomless deep,

I kiss the white foam that gambols with me,
And dash with it down to the restless sea.
Then wildly I play o'er the Ocean wide,
When Man is not near to humble my pride ;
But so fearless is he, that seldom I fail
To meet in my passage some venturous sail,
And fierce is the struggle that passes between,
And fierce my revenge is, full often, I ween,
For the daring that prompts him to wrestle and gain,
The empire I strive for—the sway o'er the main ;
But like a wild beast by the hunters at bay,
More often I crouch till He passes away,
Though wildly I rage, and my fury I vent,
Till I find, when too late, that my strength is spent.

So, something subdued in my wrath and power,
I visit your land in its wintry hour ;
And here, as I pass, I crisp the streams,
Though over them glow the faint sunbeams ;
And the fanciful pendules of ice I hold,
Where the rain-drops stay'd in their course had roll'd ;
And I patter the hail and drift the snow,
As a remnant of majesty here I show ;
While sometimes in pity I temper the brow
That fever had burnt, and send back the tide
Of health to the veins that sickness had dried,
And brace up the frame, till its twin-born, the Mind,
In gratitude loves the Wintry Wind.
But little for love or hate I try,
I do but the bidding of ONE on HIGH !

And often I creep to the chamber warm,
(One chink is enough to work the charm,)
Where the high-born and gifted, and young and fair,
Is guarded and tended with anxious care ;
But the hectic is there, and the cough so quick
Heard through the folds of the curtain thick,
And the sparkling eye, and the fingers weak,
And the heart that dares not its fulness speak ;
But here is my mission—my Icy Breath
Is the herald, and signal, and signet of Death !
Then I bluster away to a hovel low,
But quicker my work is there, I trow.

And so for a while I lord it with all,
Though weaker and weaker my power doth fall,
Till the golden Sun and the Zephyrs mild
Chase me again to the Northern Wild !

ON THE MARRIAGE OF THE QUEEN.

HAIL! to thee, Daughter of a line of Kings!
   The bridal wreath is circling thy young brow,—
And the rich pageantry of State, too, flings
   Its gorgeous trappings all around thee now.
And thronging thousands crowd Thy form to see—
   While nobles of the land, and maids high-born
Most proudly claim the right to tender thee
   Some formal service on thy bridal morn!

Hail! to thee, Daughter of old Egbert's race!
   All loving hearts are drawn more near to-day;
For they thy atmosphere of state displace,
   And roll (in thought) like a thick scroll away.
They see thee not in regal splendour shining,—
   They feel that thou art Woman, young and fair,
And joy to think, that thou this day art twining
   Love's Roses in the Crown thy head must wear!

February 10*th*, 1840.

STANZAS

WRITTEN TO ILLUSTRATE THE FRONTISPIECE TO "FRIENDSHIP'S
OFFERING" FOR 1843, REPRESENTING HER MAJESTY, H. R. H.
PRINCE ALBERT, THE PRINCE OF WALES, AND THE PRINCESS
ROYAL.

Our own loved Queen ! Each loyal heart must leap
At thoughts of Thee and Thine.   Whence is the spell
Ere early youth be pass'd, to win and hoop
The hearts of millions, who can feel, not tell
The mystic power which binds them, and doth swell
Into a holier chain than that was known
Which cold allegiance forged,—when first there fell
Upon a nation's ears thy Name—a tone
Whose syllables now have a music of their own ?

With strong illusion oft, when I have trod
Those holy fanes where rest the royal dead,
I 've thought their spirits, hovering o'er the sod,
And letter'd stones which echoed to my tread,
With viewless hand, and spirit whisper led
My thoughts to hold communion with the things
Of their far years ; and thus, methinks, I read
—As each some noble gift around Thee flings,—
Heart-greetings to thee, from Old England's greatest
      Kings.

To fancy, their cold ashes tongues do own,
And I could dream the best and wisest there,
Those who the noblest bore the heavy crown,
And yet most felt its weight—those spirits rare,
Whom death releasèd from a monarch's care,
Do greet thee with parental love and pride.
What joy ! if they with Banquo's mirror fair
—Those antique sires by wisdom's lessons tried—
Had traced thyself—thy virtues on its crystal side !

Almost a thousand years have passed away
Since the Great Alfred ruled our sea-girt land,
And shed upon its darkness the bright ray
Of his pure intellect, to there expand
And herald forth to climes beyond our strand,
A dawn which promised day.   Ah ! yes, I ween
The root *was* princely, and the tree did stand
The shock of ages ; branches brave were seen
To rise and flourish, but no flower like our fair Queen !

Norman, Plantagenet, and Tudor—those
Were grafted on that regal Saxon stem,
Which seemed, when Brunswick's fair-haired Queen
     uprose,
To gain congenial strength ; from each of them
Thou dost inherit as a peerless gem
Some glorious attribute : Plantagenet
(Who twice was crown'd with England's diadem)
Bequeath'd his " lion heart," for never yet
Was soul so firm in such a lovely casket set.

It is an Hour of Rest,—sweet, holy, dear,—
No Crown doth press upon that forehead fair,
But HE, the chosen of thy heart, is near,
To whose fond love and ever anxious care
Thyself was given.   Granted is the prayer
That rose from millions, when thou didst select
That noble nature, in whose lustre ne'er
Could even envy's factious breath detect
One spot or shade to darken his high intellect !

But 'tis not only Mind, or poet's gift,
Or skill o'er painter's pencil, or such powers
Which do our hearts in reverent homage lift
Unto THE PRINCE, howe'er life's fleeting hours
Are winged and hallowed by the lavish showers
The Mind can scatter from its countless store :
All these are His and Thine, of both the dowers—
And yet of love heartfelt and flowing o'er,
The generous noble heart, and kindly words win more.

It is an Hour of Rest—sweet, holy, dear,
In which affection's fount is all unsealed,
Whose gushing waters, deep, and bright, and clear,
Find here pure channels for their course revealed.
Oh, what a wealth of tenderness concealed
Dwells in the fond caress and circling arm !
A balm by which fate's deepest wounds are healed.
Flowers at your feet ! fit emblems,—would a charm
They had to overgrow all weeds that sting and harm !

F

Thy First-born clinging to a mother's knee
In all of infant beauty's untaught grace!
With Fancy's eye a smile of joy I see,
And thoughts beyond her baby years I trace,
Rejoicing that the brother of her race
Hath ta'en away, with firm but gentle right,
The Shadow of a crown that Time must place,
And cares, and heavy sceptre, from her sight,—
Now flowers and gems alone shall press those tresses
          bright!

How proud the title, beauteous Boy, is thine,
Borne by full many of the great of old,
Belonging only to that regal line
Whose sires are thine!   Oh, dead or marble-cold
The heart that does not fond remembrance hold
Of him, " the Black " of Poitiers'—Cressy's fields,
Boy conqueror—who won, as true as bold,
The filial motto England never yields,
From wild Bohemia's brave old king for *both* your shields !

How rare the host revealed by memory's light,
Who bore the title England's Heir must claim !
And bore it like a star upon the night
Of those dark ages when the warrior's name
Almost alone was trumpeted by fame.
But happier omens than star-gazing seers
(Who in those days such oracles became)
E'er conjured 'mid their frantic hopes and fears,
Young Prince, shed influence sure upon thy opening years !

God grant you life, long life, ye Royal Pair!
Not all unselfish is the prayer I know,
That we may bask beneath the sunshine rare
Of your pure influence—your children grow
Beneath its high protection—till they show
The pattern of a princely house.   And may
The gathering drifts of many winters' snow
Fall gently o'er you, ere the last sad day
Leaves to a child of Yours Old England's realms to sway!

June, 1842.

A DEFENCE OF LONDON:

Nor live in London!   Wherefore not? come tell.
Think ye that Poesy alone can dwell
Within a rustic cot, where zephyr brings,
Upon his treasure-laden, perfumed wings,
Tribute from every flower ; or where the sky
Seems, in its ether's clear intensity,
A loftier arch than spans our crowded town,
    Whose Age is Poetry ?—A well so vast
That ever self-supplying, it has grown
    Exhaustless in its wealth.   Present and Past
(And a bright Future, that to poets' eyes
Doth as a poet's glorious vision rise,)
Alike impregnate London's "cloud-capp'd towers"
With Poesy's own soul.   Swiftly the hours
Bring death to us, but this immortal is
    Even on earth:—let mighty man o'erthrow
Each monumental fane, it is not his
    To find oblivion's fount,—nor does he know
    The secret to destroy ;—even as now,
Each broken stone a ready tongue would find,
    Wherewith to wisely charm all those who will

With open ears to listen.   Oh ! not blind
  To Nature's loveliness are they who still
May love the Regal City ;—and perchance,
Contrast may so a rural scene enhance,
  That they most feel it, and best mark the links
Which bind in one bright, universal chain,
  All Poesy :—from the parched blade that drinks
The welcome dew, through the vast myriad train
Of things and thoughts, till at the last one feels
Most rich the lore the city's haunt reveals.
" Man made it ! "   True : but caught by tripping speech.
  Ye do forget the Greater Architect
Who formed his workman, Man.   I do beseech
  Ye, marvel not that Poets should select
Old London for a home ;—true bards will own
The inspiration of the busy town.
Have not the greatest dwelt within her walls—
Mix'd with their fellow-men—obey'd the calls
Of such good fellowship ? Ay, even they,
The Imperial Two, who jointly sway
The realms of Mind ! (as in the Roman world,
Two eagle banners were at once unfurl'd.)
The Peerless Bard, whose wise and deathless strain
Was wealth the richest of the Maiden's reign—
Who in the town not only learn'd to read
  The book of human nature through and through,
But painted sunny clime or flowery mead,
  And sprite, or fay, with Poesy's own hue.
And He of Paradise, who 'mid the strife
Of civil discord led the student's life ;

When none there seem'd with wings that e'en could dare
To track the soarings of his pinions rare ;
The mighty mind its own defence and shield,
'Mid all the ills that " evil days " could yield !
These were the denizens of our great town—
They trod familiar paths that we have known :
So let them sanctify the Place, and teach
A wise rejoinder to your thoughtless speech !

ON THE FATE OF "THE PRESIDENT"
STEAM-SHIP.

Is there not One the mournful tale to tell,
  And paint the picture with Truth's lasting hue ?
Must sicken'd fancy, shuddering, vainly dwell
  On the gaunt horrors conjured to our view—
Haply unreal all, though truth-like each—
Mocking the hearts that truth shall never reach ?

Hope fades away, and now her sweet words sink
  To a mere soulless echo; while Despair
Is wrestling with the hearts that trembling shrink
  From his embrace. Must we no longer dare
To trust bright hope, that still will fondly cling
To each wild chance of our imagining ?

Answer, old Ocean, from thy caverns deep !
  Answer, ye summer waves, that harmless now
Sparkle beneath the sunbeams !   Do ye keep
  Records of your dread doings ; or avow
Your right, with majesty supreme and cold,
To the red tribute ye have claim'd of old ?

Ocean, thou art not all a monarch !   Man
   Has half-subdued thee to his rebel will.
Must the dread struggle last for ever ?   Can
   His triumph swell by mightier victories still ?
In God's right hand an instrument art thou,
But to man's mind God may thy greatness bow!

Answer, sea-breezes !—that with healthy breath
   Kiss the pale cheek of sickness or of care—
Will *ye* the tale unfold of woe and death ?
   Do ye no message to the mourners bear ?
Gaily ye come, ruffling each leaf and flower;
Have ye forgot the tempest's darker hour ?

And thou, pure sky !—whose dome of azure bright
   Seems but to canopy a smiling world ;
And wakeful stars ! that pierce the veil of night,
   In that stern hour were all your glories furl'd ?
Or did ye weave of them a funeral pall,
O'er the unknown, unpictured scene to fall ?

Wind, Ocean, Sky, I ask of ye anew,
   Will ye not cast one ray to light the gloom
Of blank obscurity ?   *Do* we but view
   Above, a pall ?—*is* ocean but a tomb ?—
And *did* the winds the requiem perform,
'Mid the wild fury of the raging storm ?

Between Ye is the triumph—take it all !
   Hopes rudely crush'd—affection's sever'd ties—
The widow's, parent's, orphan's tears that fall,
   Racking the hearts that break not—tears that rise
From that deep well of bitterness and woe,
Where human agonies are born and grow !

Is it not said that in this real world,
   He who descends to a deep pit can see,
E'en at mid-day, the stars above ?   And, hurl'd
   Into this well of grief, oh ! may it be
That heavenly light shall cheer the mourners' way,
O'er which cold death has veil'd earth's brightest ray!

June, 1841.

THE UMPIRES OF THE COMBAT.

Dark-Eyed daughters of the land,
Where young Beauty's cheeks are fann'd
By the breeze, which odour steals,
And the fragrant theft reveals,
Coming from the orange flower,
To the ladies' shady bower!
Children of that southern clime,
Chronicled in olden time
As the land of rich romance,
And of beauty's witching glance;
Where the Goths and Moorish race
Struggled for the regal place;
Where the Cid once fought and bled,
And—oh! strange the story—wed!
Daughters of the land that seems
To northern fancy, bright as dreams;
Where the sunshine over all
On the generous soil doth fall;
Where the olives rich do dwell,
And the luscious grape doth swell,
Till the sparkling amber wine,
Born but of the clinging vine,

Is an offering fit and sweet,
When the great and lovely meet.
Land of beauty—sunny Spain,
Girt by mountains and the main ;
Seemingly most blest of Heaven,
Yet by murderous discord riven !
Ladies, from your balcony,
Why look ye down with anxious eye,
Is it for a lover nigh ?

No ! a whisper floats to me,
And I grieve that it should be.
Gentle ladies, gaze no more
On the wounded Matadore,
Or the noble Bull which now
Madden'd—writhing—lies below.
Remnant of a barbarous stage,
Blot it from the present age ;
Or if ye cannot sway the throng,
Be not Ye the crowd among !

A SONG OF THE TREES.

———◆———

" A song for ourselves ! " cried the old Oak Tree,
" *I* will begin with my pedigree.
Nothing am I degenerate :
Not like some boasters who but prate
Of the lordly line
Whence they decline,
More surely to prove
How far the remove
From the ' Rodolf of their race.'
But no decay in me ye trace
From the olden sires who long ago
Wav'd their green arms to and fro
O'er the Druid priests who there
Sacrificed with song and prayer.
I am young—and yet my brothers
   Fell, a century ago,
'Neath the axe that levell'd others,
   Ripe, like them, to brave the foe.
Axe and hammer, saw and hatchet,
   If ye will to dream the sound,
Listen ! Fancy's ear may catch it,
   All our Island booming round,

While Old England's mighty Fleet
Rose Old England's foes to meet.
Listen to the grinding saw,

   Listen to the hammer's stroke ;
Think without a speck or flaw,

   How the noble vessels broke
From their lashings—ocean-seeking,
Like a bird from bondage breaking.
Many an oaken plank was stain'd,
When the blood of heroes rain'd :
Some were shiver'd by the ball,
In the hour when brave men fall,
But they always bore away
The tatter'd flag in proud array !
Oh ! how fast do memories throng,
Which I *could* weave into song ;
But the chorus join with me
Ere another minstrelsy.

   Voices we have beneath the blue sky,

   Hark to our singing ! " The wind rushes by !
Said the Pine, " Come, let there float
O'er the waves for me a note,
Ere shall close the haughty strain
That tells *our* doings on the main.
First think how my resin blood
Keeps the proud ship taut and good.
Pitch, and tar, and turpentine,—
Am not I a goodly vine ?
Mine the gallant mast uprearing,
And the snowy canvas bearing ;

Though, perchance, to bend and quiver
When the winds the white sails shiver,
Yet upsprings my tapering form
Again to meet the growing storm,
To struggle for the ocean path,
To brave the tempest's maddened wrath,
That tears me like a fragile reed,
That flings me like the ocean weed,
To lie—in majesty no more—
   A log upon the waters !
Yet e'en, ere such an hour be o'er,
   To Earth's fair sons and daughters
Have I done service.   Manhood's arm
Has clasp'd me in its dread alarm.
And while was struggling Life with Death,
I 've sav'd for Life the parting breath.
So for the Pine a glowing song,
  And for the chorus find a tongue.
    Voices we have beneath the blue sky,
    Hark to our singing !"   The wind rushes by !

Now a full deep voice is heard,
Listen to the Laurel's word ;
Haughty though the tone may sound,
Mournfully it echoes round.

" Of me they weave the deathless crown,
Won by deeds of high renown ;
But I who press the victor's brow
Ambition's secrets often know ;

And I have thought the poison-fruits
That from my sap great Nature shoots
(That sap supplying glossy sheen
To hide the fruit with evergreen)
Were no poor emblem of the end
To which Ambition's struggles tend.
Ye mark the few who reach the goals,
Not those for whom Oblivion rolls ;
Not them who fainting in the race,
Though dower'd with souls deserving place,
Miss some small accident of fate
To ope Success, and show them great !
And when the wreath at last is won,
How often I but rest upon
The marble bust !—no teeming brow
Where thought should kindle—genius glow ;
Which had I clasp'd when life was there,
I could have turn'd the wand of Care,
And back recall'd the dormant tide
Of healthful joys and honest pride.
But let the Laurel join your song,
And for the chorus find a tongue.
  Voices we have beneath the blue sky,
  Hark to our singing !"   The wind rushes by !

Then the Elm, in sonorous tone,
Made a fitful vision known.

" I am young—an Elm Tree's youth ;
  Yet behold that white-hair'd man,

Ere his little life began,
I was blooming, and, in sooth,
Listen'd to the lover's vow,
And beheld the rosy glow
On the village beauty's cheek,
When his grandsire dared to speak
Of the Eden here below,
Which two loving hearts may know;
Old the tale, as old can be,
The Paradise each heart can see,
Yet for it made new and fair,
With an Eve or Adam there!
Round about my spreading girth
Children frolick'd in their mirth,
Gossips told the village-tale—
Politicians stay'd to rail,
'Neath the pleasant friendly shade
That my spreading branches made.
But beneath the scythe of Death
Already have they yielded breath;
Or full soon (for soon to me
Seems the half a century)
They must bow beneath the yoke
Of the never-failing stroke.
Yet when I hear the mournful chime
Chronicling this work of Time,
From the fibres of my root
To where the tender leaflets shoot,
I can feel a shudder creep,
And a pang of anguish sweep!

For by these our words reveal'd
We have sympathies conceal'd,
Which are the unseen links that make
That chain a Poet cannot break,
When dreaming that the world is nought
And all the Universe but Thought.
Brothers ! to some it is ordain'd
To form the crown that Genius gain'd ;
To some, to bind their limbs together,
To shelter man from wind and weather,
Or bear him over·raging seas
Inwoven in life's destinies.
But brother Oak, to you and me
Death also hath one stern decree !
When nothing but the dull cold clay
Remains, as if to warn away,
Half with a solemn awe and dread,
Half from a loathing of the dead,
Those whom in life it lov'd the best
Thus mutely asking earth's last rest ;
When to the lip decay has sprung,
Where yesterday the lover clung,
With the bewilder'd tenderness
Of love's most passionate excess,
We, shapen'd to the COFFIN's mould,
The wreck of mortal form enfold ! "

Fainter now grew every word,
And the chorus was not heard,
Till beneath the deep blue sky,
But the Wind was rushing by !

STANZAS.

As down the stream the hours glide on
  Beneath Time's shadowy wing,
I feel that whatsoe'er it seem,
  LIFE *is* an earnest thing !

I must not cast my anchor 'mong
  The hidden rocks and shoals,
O'er which, beside its flower-crown'd bank,
  Youth's limpid river rolls.

I can but snatch with trembling hand
  Some blossoms from the shore,
The while my bark sails swiftly on,
  Though we return no more.

Yet, lit by Memory's moon-like beam,
  Youth, rising to our sight,
Perchance looks fairer from afar
  Than by intenser light.

For blacken'd ruins bleak and cold,
  That rise from out the flowers,
May take a form of mournful grace
  In Memory's moonlight hours !

On—on—the stream is widening fast,
  We ask for Fortune's breeze
To fill our sails, and bear us soon
  To Life's more open seas.

And now we seek the Star above,
  That guides us on aright ;
Though lending to each mortal eye
  Perchance a different light.

Still to One haven does it lead,
  And ever, as we gaze,
It grows more bright, with Heaven's light,
  And wide expanding rays.

Ah ! better by the star above
  To steer with trusting heart,
Than bend a downward eye to mark
  A worldling's crowded chart !

Th' experience of no other mind
  Precisely suits our own ;
By light before, and silvery wake,
  Our pathway may be known.

On—on—we find a few stray gems
  From wisdom's treasure keep ;
But here we cannot anchor drop,
  The waters are too deep !

We seize the gems, and wreathe them with
   The flowers of love and youth,
And fear no ill, though waves run high,
   If at the helm sits Truth.

Truth !—that still dazzles weakest eyes,
   Although to it is given
To teach us, by its radiant light,
   To know the light of Heaven !

THE BLIND GIRL'S LAMENT.

It is not that I cannot see
  The birds and flowers of spring,
'Tis not that beauty seems to me
  A dreamy unknown thing :
It is not that I cannot mark
  The blue and sparkling sky,
Nor ocean's foam, nor mountain's peak,
  That e'er I weep or sigh.

They tell me that the birds, whose notes
  Fall rich, and sweet, and full,—
That these I listen to and love,
  Are not all beautiful !
They tell me that the gayest flowers
  Which sunshine ever brings,
Are not the ones I know so well,
  But strange and scentless things !

My little brother leads me forth
  To where the violets grow ;
His gentle, light, yet careful step,
  And tiny hand I know.

My mother's voice is soft and sweet,
　　Like music on my ear ;
The very atmosphere seems love,
　　When these to me are near.

My father twines his arms around,
　　And draws me to his breast,
To kiss the poor blind helpless girl,
　　He says he loves the best.
'Tis then I ponder unknown things,
　　It may be—weep or sigh,
And think how glorious it must be
　　To meet Affection's eye !

1838

THE THREE FRIENDS.

THERE were Three Friends—that is to say,
They were men meeting every day ;
Grasping each other's hands with earnest pressure
Upon the Mart, or in the hours of leisure.

The Eldest had a large and finely-tempered heart,
Thought a few thoughts in which the world had not a part,
And, as the mountains are the first to win
A dawning glory ere the day begin,
He saw to trace his life-chart on a plan
Of simple grandeur meet for such a man.

His acts oft puzzled worldlings, who, you know,
Bat-like, are blinded by the noon-day glow
Of deeds to which they cannot find the clue
Of double motive or a selfish view.
And yet as mountain sun-crowns downwards creep
Till o'er the plain the generous day-beams sweep,
So from the height of his great soul were caught
Some peerless lessons by example taught.

"But," says the reader, "to these Three Great Friends,
I cannot see which way your story tends."

Patience :—and yet perchance when all is told,
Meaning or moral you may not behold !
Of station, fortune, equal all had been,
But to the younger two came losses unforeseen.
Generous and prompt, the First with open hand
Made free his fortune to their joint command ;
Saying, " It is a gift or loan, it matters not,
According to the chances of your future lot."
A test of friendship bravely, nobly borne ;
But though the theme be much less trite and worn,
It is almost as hard—I own, not quite—
To take with grace, as to bestow aright
Favours like this ; which try mind-metal more
Than shielding life with life amid the battle's roar.

One was profuse of thanks ; yet you might see
He bit his lip half-peevishly,
And to his cheeks the chafed and feverish blood
Sent fitfully its tell-tale flood.

The Other said, " God bless thee !" fervently ;
" God knows I would have done the same for thee."

And several signs stood out in strong relief
To mark the Twain ;—but, to be brief,
The One a slave, in struggling to escape,
Broke up his household gods of every shape
To melt them—in his heart—into one figure rude
Of monstrous mien, which he called Gratitude :
Until, self-tortured by his hideous guest,
Day brought no peace, and night no rest !

The Other one walked upright as when he
First knew his friend in all equality :
There was no servile crouching ; no revoke
Of differing thoughts he once had freely spoke
(For e'en as discords harmony may make,
So kindred minds some different views may take).
The only chain the gold 'twixt them had wrought
Drew them more near, and dearer friendship brought.
" God knows I would have done the same for thee !"
" *I* know he would have done as much for me !"
Was felt—not said—by each respectively.
An unsung music to themselves most dear,
As one may silent read a page, not hear.

The writhing slave knew nought of such sweet peace ;
His visits shorten, and at last they cease.
As for the Lender, if his thoughts be told,
He mourns to lose a friend, and not his gold.
Unto the Other once he said, " Your words are true :
You 've tested me ; but I have tested you !
It pains my heart to know *he* could not comprehend
The rights and pleasures of a faithful friend."

" It chances," said the Third, " that you and I
Do understand each other perfectly.
But frankly tell me, do not you opine
That, out of every hundred, ninety-nine
Of poor mankind do not know how
Either t' accept a favour or a boon bestow ?

No matter what on Friendship's Shrine th' oblation,
They shrink in horror from an Obligation !
So little are the ties of brotherhood
Between Earth's children understood,
So few who seem such thoughts to understand,
That I could count, upon the fingers of one hand,
With whom I know such bonds might be,
And give or take all equally,
Without disturbance of our self-respect,
Or some regret the curious might detect."

" 'Tis very sad !" the First one sighing cried,
" God's gifts we most unequally divide :
How shall we teach one human brotherhood ?"

" Trust God ! and trust the might of doing good !"
The Other answer'd, " There's a dawn draws near
(May eyes grow stronger ere the noon appear,
For some I know that not e'en now can bear
Truth's struggling beams that pierce this murky air)
Why, 'tis a wholesome sign, you will aver,
That even You and I can thus confer !"

THE QUESTION.

" It is hard, in this state of things, not to conceive that the time among us, at least, is an essentially unpoetic one—one which, whatever may be the worth of its feelings, finds no utterance for them in melodious words."—
Quarterly Review, Sept., 1842.

WHY doth no Poet rise to be THE BARD
Of this most pregnant Age ?   And proving thus
Th' interpreter and oracle of Truth ;
To stand upon the pedestal of Fame ;
To be enshrinéd in the hearts of men ;
To be a Name ; the Symbol of a Power
Acknowledged, and so spread, that infants now,
And all their future far posterity,
May know it for a tone, like those Great Few
Familiar Ones—an ignorance of which
The memory feebly holds ?   Why doth no Bard
Arise to be the link for which we call ?
The link in that strange chain which ages forge
To bind—and so bequeath—the power of Thought,
Which makes the world not all a savage wild,
And man the rich inheritor he is ?
Why doth no Bard arise to teach, that Truth
Is Poetry, and Poetry is Truth ?

· A simple phrase ; and yet that chain is wrought
Of giant minds that did thus simply teach.

Unto my humble thought, it seems as sure
The Bard *will* come, as that the nicely-poised
And whirling earth careering round the sun,
Will give us summer fruit and winter snow ;
But each in season.   These are ponderous Times,
In which things, thoughts, and feelings, swell beyond
The accustomed olden channel of trite words,
And so o'erflowing, sink again within
The mind from whence they rose ; but—to enrich
It more, and feed the parent springs, which shall,
In their allotted time, burst forth, and delve
A pathway for themselves !   Doth not our tongue
Grow richer with the wealth of mind ?   Men coin
The words they want ; and when they have a thing
They find expression for it.   So the Bard
Will come.   We have the wealth of " feelings " high ;
Is not their " utterance " near ?

1842.

A BANQUET SONG.

Sound the harp again to-night,
Rich the strain as ever,
Let the goblet sparkling bright
Pass before we sever.
Glass of Venice, give us such,
Shivering at a traitor's touch !
Honoured guests are at the board,
'Tis to them the wine is poured,
They the famed in martial story,
Wearing well-earned wreaths of glory !
 This the pledge ! Come, fill the cup,
 See the wine is sparkling up,
 As if rubies bright and rare,
 Melted in the goblet were.

Sons of Genius at the board,
Now to them the wine is poured.
In their own "land's language" they
Teach what cannot fade away.
Genius of immortal birth
Fame immortal leaves on earth,
Winning, on the glowing page,
Its eternal heritage.

This the pledge !   Come, fill the cup,
See the wine is sparkling up,
As if rubies bright and rare,
Melted in the goblet were.

Mark ye not a flashing eye ?
Young Ambition lingers by ;
Let us lead such spirits on,
Ere our minstrel's task be done.
Think, 'tis not the tempest's blast
Brings the flow'ret forth at last ;
And the fruits most prized and rare
Ask the Summer's genial care.
Then the seeds of Genius cherish,
Let them not neglected perish,
Let them bask beneath the rays
Of affection and of praise.
    To such spirits fill the cup
    See the wine is sparkling up,
    As if rubies bright and rare,
    Melted in the goblet were.

Once again the wine is poured,
Beauty is around the board !
Let the sparkling torrent flow,
Every lip will drain it now.
Heroes even smile to own
How they Beauty's rule have known,
Vassal slaves before her bending,
Only sad the bondage ending.

What were young Ambition's dream,
Did not Beauty o'er him beam,
Seeming like a prize alone
For the most deserving one ?
Ask the gifted—for they know,
And in faithful records show,
Telling of the lonely lot
Of a life where love is not.
    Glass of Venice ! give us such,
    Traitors dare not brave its touch ;
    Had we Cleopatra's pearl
    In the goblet now to hurl,
    Though the draught were richer still,
    Not a heart could warmer thrill !
    Pour the wine, and fill high up,
    Every lip will drain the cup !

1840.

THE RAILWAY WHISTLE.

THE Whistle! I love it—its shrill note—hark!
  Hath a music unto my soul
Richer and sweeter than throstle or lark,
  For matin could ever troll.
Each day doth it teach-me, by some dream,
  For I hear it a score of times,
If I choose to watch for the feathery Steam
  Or list to Its gladdening chimes.

Hish—sh—there's a Train! which hath come with a
  To rival the carrier dove,   . [speed
Mocking the limbs of the racing steed,
  On its mission of peace and love.
It bringeth glad words from—some sick friend,
  And they are so newly writ,
Ye forget the terrors that time might send,
  For the ink is pallid yet!

A Lover hath journey'd a hundred miles,
  And it's nothing at all to do,
For a kiss perhaps, and a few sweet smiles,
  A meeting, a parting, a fond adieu.

He hath stolen the end of a toiling day,
　But is back ere the morning beams,
With his wealth, of memories dear to lay
　On the shrine of his waking dreams !

Knowledge hath travelled—(the People's I mean)
　Packed up in huge paper bales,
To work out a marvel, more great I ween,
　Than the wonders of fairy tales.
For the wizard deeds of former years,
　But small admiration claim,
And a Wizard Servant here appears,
　That putteth them all to shame !

He knoweth to work by the Press and the Boat,
　By the Loom, and the Iron Road ;
And I love the Whistle's shrieking note
　As a messenger from God,
Better than lark or throstle's song,
　As, telling more than they,
In its own distinct, suggestive tongue,
　Of the dawn of a Better Day !

THE SENATOR'S BRIDE.

Go, Love ! I would not have thee stay
  A Loiterer by my side ;
Nor purchase one soul-thrilling word
  By forfeit of thy pride.
Go, Love ! thy peers (if peers thou hast)
  Seek counsel from thy tongue ;
I would not they should deem my kiss
  Upon thy lips yet hung.

I would not have thee passion's slave,
  A loftier hope is mine ;
It is, that reason should approve
  Each ardent thought of thine.
I would be still thine only love,
  And yet thy best-loved friend ;
So speech may be but thought aloud,
  And all emotions blend.

I thank thee, thou hast let me read
  The shadows on thy brow,
And comprehend the anxious thoughts
  That struggling Man must know.
It is this confidence that e'en
  In absence is my pride—
That lets me smile at jealous fears,
  And bid thee from my side.

THE MIGHTY DEAD.

"The dead but sceptred sovereigns, who still rule
Our spirits from their urns."—BYRON.

ERE beauteous Earth had ever felt decay,
  When man first knew it for a resting-place,
And this, the new-born world, untroubled lay
  Upon the bosom of unfathomed space,—
The Dead were not! Yet Purest Spirit breathed
His will Omnipotent, and It was wreathed
With the first tree, and herb, and bright young flowers
Startled to life in Eden's sunny bowers.
And this was heard in the first joyous song
  The lark uplifted to the throne on high,
And their fixed laws were willed to last thus long,
  " While the Young Earth fulfils her destiny!"
And Nature never hath had sight or sound,
Where this pure essence was not felt around.

But most it ruleth in the heart of man;
  For Mind was chosen as the instrument
On earth to work all changes, and began
  The God-deputed task, when first was blent
With clay this essence pure. This was the seal
  To mark mankind from each less wondrous thing:
" Man shall to man his inmost thoughts reveal,
  And, dying, shall bequeath them; and shall fling
H 2

A subtle spirit, which can never die,
O'er the wide path of far futurity."
This is the quenchless light that ever burns,
And so " the dead are rulers from their urns."

The earth grows old, but still no wrinkles show,
    To mar the lustre of her blooming face;
And yet the very dust we trample low
    Doth point its moral to the human race.
Earth is one mighty grave of human clay,
But Mind immortal doth not pass away;
It is the monument which doth outlive
All that the sculptor's art can ever give.
And through these monuments we do converse
With our dead friends, while they perchance rehearse
The heart-throbs we have known.   Or counsel seek
From the rare scrolls where our dead teachers speak,
And win obedience still.   Are we not led
By the just influence of the Mighty Dead ?
Are not such bonds of sympathy more true
Than the frail links the living rend in two ?
What though they lived a thousand years ago,—
Are they not spirit-friends through weal and woe ?
And can we look around, and fail to trace
Material records of a bygone race !
Is it not theirs, our thoughts and deeds to school,
The inner and the outer world to rule ?
The monarchs these, to whom our homage turns,—
The Dead, " who rule our Spirits from their urns !"

        1841.

THE BEST CHAMBER.

I stood within those Lordly Halls,
   I will not breathe the name,
Though it hath echoed round the world,
   In varied notes of fame.
I will not tell the word would point
   The race, and place, I mean.
For human hearts know Truer Truths
   Than dates and names, I ween.

Yet there 's a half endowed mind,
   The man who talks and reads,
Heaps fact on fact—thinks knowledge lies
   In chronicling of Deeds :
Deeds ! that may stand like warning towers,
   Yet little do they teach,
Unless we track the burning path
   Which led from each to each !

For such we leave the " lying " page,
   Immortal Raleigh named,*
Whose clinging satire to this day
   Th' Historian's task has shamed.

---

* " Give me that volume of lies," said Sir Walter Raleigh, while confined in the Tower, and asking for a book of History.

Shamed—though the Poet thanks him well
    For that cold skeleton,
Which He can warm to life, and mould
    A form of beauty on.

I stood within those Ancient Walls,
    The " show-house," fine to see ;
Through stately rooms, 'neath lorldly domes,
    We passed on merrily.
Smiling, to think how much alike
    Such places seem to be,
Bare boards, though meet for strangers' feet,
    Chairs covered carefully.

For o'er the floors the sunlight pours,
    High from each western pane ;
The quivering trees in the balmy breeze,
    Their trembling shadows rain ;
The song of birds, and flowers' breath,
    Proclaim mid-summer days,
The Lord is where the Senate band
    A nation's sceptre sways.

A few brief weeks in Autumn time,
    When grouse or partridge falls,
Make up the space of time he spares
    His old ancestral halls.
In mansions four by turns he dwells—
    (What new ground Fancy treads,
I see the throng who have no home
    Wherein to lay their heads !)

Along the wall old pictures rest,
 From many a master hand ;
Vandyke and Kneller, Reynolds, too,
 Present a goodly band
Of stately dames, and warriors grim,
 And courtiers smooth of tongue,
And some whose deathless fame and name
 To history belong.

But mid this Painted Pedigree,
 Gleams one surpassing face
Of young ripe beauty—and the form
 Which Lely loved to trace.
The mistress of a King she was,
 From her till now descends
Some beauty, and a title high,
 Which with as high ones blends !

The menial, who with courteous pride
 The Cicerone plays,
Points out the favourite, fair and frail,
 The theme of poets' lays.
" Her son first Duke—the likeness great—"
 So doth our guide declare—
" Indeed the present Ladies —— Blank
 Have just that auburn hair."

In sacred quiet rest her dust—
 God ! keep her soul, I pray.
Be sure She did not fail on earth
 Her penalty to pay.

But oh, it is a curious thing,
   And might a cynic make
To note the strange distorted forms
   That human pride will take !

So passed we on through many rooms,
   Each had its name, I trow ;
" We 're in," our guide, explaining cried,
   " The Guest's ' Best Chamber ' now.
For ages 'twas their Graces' own,
   So used in years long past ;
Here five great Dukes were born, and here
   Did seven breathe their last.
But since—you know the tale no doubt—
   That dreadful suicide,
The family dislike the room,
   And none will here abide."

Instant, there flash'd within my soul
   A sort of solemn light,
By which obedient Memory
   Unrolled her pictures bright ;
For well I knew the storied deeds
   Of this same titled race,
And in that room for me there dwelt
   The genius of the Place !

Through floors and walls there seemed to come
   A mighty spirit-band
That grouped themselves as at the wave
   Of some commander's hand.

On passed they like the shifting scenes
  Of Banquo's mirror true,
His of the future—mine the past,
  I will recall a few.

The despot Fashion (its gay crown
  The cap adorn'd with bells)
Rules even Vice whose deep dark wave
  By fashion ebbs and swells.
The Gamester's base degraded life
  Not now the thing to ape,
The gods of avarice and chance
  Have ta'en another shape.

But scarcely three-score years ago,
  Our nobles great and high
Played cleverly the painted cards,
  Were practised with the die ;
E'en Woman with a trembling lip,
  Flushed cheek, but drooping lid,
With jewelled fingers clutched the gold,
  Or—death-like anguish hid.

Such scenes, that time, were common things
  Within this Mansion fair,
Though Fashion lent her gaudy cloak
  The leper-spots were there.
'Twas then there was a Merchant-prince,
  Unmeasured wealth he swayed,
Who as a highly-honoured guest
  Here with his daughter stayed.

Some talk there 'd been, some treaty framed
　By which this maid should wed,
And for a title barter gold,
　The greedy fathers said.
True, hers was vile plebeian blood ;
　Yet one had played his part,
The lordly Heir had warmly woo'd
　And she 'd—a woman's heart !

Father and son both wanted gold :
　Whence sprung the Gamester's thought
To win the gold—not take the wife ?
　The web was duly wrought.
The beggar'd merchant paid the debt—
　His " honour " he must keep :
A kinder bridegroom found the girl—
　'Twas sweet with Death to sleep !

And in This Room died these great lords.—
　The first delirium rack'd ;
He raved of dice—of title-deeds,
　And cards with cunning pack'd.
The second—did no spectre walk
　To palsy him with dread ;
No thorns spring through the down where lay
　His coronetted head ?
Did not *her* lips once bloom again,
　And in the death-hour hiss,
To pay him back a withering curse
　For every lying kiss ?

The Scene grows dim, it melts away ;
  Another I behold,
A youthful bride and beautiful,
  A husband stern and cold.
Deep love had warm'd her free, fresh soul,
  Maturing heart and mind :
Alas, alas ! but not for him
  To whom her fate they bind !

The deadly poison of false words
  Had been for her prepared,
And subtly poured, till she believed
  The thing that they declared.
Letters kept back—false messages—
  The tale so old and dark ;
Yet why did she, by all that 's pure,
  Unto another hark ?
Why did she act the deadly sin
  Of wedding without love—
A deed that says, " I am all strength,
  Temptation all above ?"

Be merciful in judging her,
  And her unhappy fate ;
Much teaching had she to unlearn
  Which she unlearn'd too late.
Of all the evils Women bear,
  Crushed as they are by wrong,
The deepest are the lessons false
  They hear from every tongue ;

Till feelings that they cannot crush,
 For very shame they hide,
And bury pure and holy thoughts
 Beneath an icy pride ;
And where an earthy seal is set
 In natures base and low,
They grow the heartless things they seem :
 With her it was not so.

Not *thus* she erred—though in despair,
 And lashed by Woman's pride
To soar above the scornful one,
 She did become a bride :
To find—how soon !—the vanity
 Of worldly pomp and show,
And to discover the foul cheat
 That doomed her life to woe.

To find that he, her lord, had known
 The falsehood now confess'd ;
Yet nightly in this very Room
 Her loathèd couch she press'd.
Here tears rained fast ; though afterwards
 Hers was that arid grief,
To which the tears that will not spring
 Would be such sweet relief.

Here watched she o'er a sickly babe,
 Heart-racked by dull despair ;
Seeking to fan Life's flickering spark
 With almost frantic care.

She knew she loved with Mother's love,
  A joy worth woe to win ;
But did not know that Little Life
  Was all 'twixt her and sin !

All—and enough.   Her warm deep heart
  Was filled such thoughts among ;
It scarce had want of other love,
  Not room for any wrong.
The barrier, holy in its strength,
  Lay shiver'd at her feet :
The mourning garb and coffin small
  This "passage" may complete.

Her Life had now a darker phase,
  Kaleidoscopic change,
Where shone two starlike Memories,
  In truth an union strange.
Yet though like double stars distinct,
  Each love lent love a light,
And by their rays in her sad heart
  But showed surrounding night !

Did yearning for the Dead wear out,
  As God in mercy wills ?
Or—Absence not unfrequently
  A friendly part fulfils—
Did the one Other Memory grow
  A flame to scorch, not light,
Ere Circumstance, with "crutch-like rod,"
  Brought Him before her sight ?

Him she had wronged !   I do believe
  In souls so finely strung,
There even from their darkest faults
  Some goodness may be wrung ;
Some stepping-stone of high intent
  Be found, which led astray,
And lured them on in trance-like flight
  Through Error's cloudy way:

Him she had wronged !   What penitence,
  What abject humble words,
Could best attune to peace again
  His heart's yet jarring chords ?
One interview—one—one—no more ;
  'Twas granted him at length :
A thousand angels her should guard
  Who trieth thus her strength !

Struggles more fierce than life with death ;
  Hair silver'd in a night ;
And not One holy love to keep
  Her Woman's heart aright !
She fled—and Shame's funereal pall
  But heralded her bier :
No portrait of her decks these walls ;
  Her tomb ?   It is not here !

Brief chronicles ! and others rise
  The crowding page to fill
Of heart-enacted tragedies
  That shame the player's skill.

On—on—the phantom band press through
  This gaily gorgeous Room,
With pulses bared, like those who found
  In Eblis Hall their doom.

The last one comes, and wearing still
  A look of princely pride ;
But through that mask there stands confess'd,
  The daring Suicide !
The trappings now of wealth and state
  Are all transparent things,
Through which are seen the festering wounds
  Of human passions' stings !

Ambition—Love—Religion—which
  Mind-master did he meet ?
For these the springs which oftenest shake
  Strong Reason from her seat.
What dull'd the keen delicious sense
  That mere existence seems,
And taught his soul to wander dark
  Mid foul and charnel dreams ?
What changed for him far-seeing Hope
  To corpse-like blind Despair ?
For outward blessings fortune held
  Him in especial care.

Imagination's glowing self,
  Kindled by Suff'ring's torch,
Can only trace an outline dim,
  Can enter but the porch,

Not scan the gloomy temple, where
    The souls distraught abide,
In those preluding hours which lead
    To maniac Suicide!

No matter what his secret grief ;
    On earth heart-griefs are rife
Which from the broken spirit press
    Our clinging love of life.
Griefs for which Hope has not a word
    To cheer with cheating love,
And Time that only could be kind
    Seems all too slow to move !

Enough, enough ! the dream is o'er,
    The phantoms glide away ;
I hear a voice in arch reproof—
    " You no attention pay,
This chair—the gift of George the Third,
    Indeed, he says, it 's true ;
And see that glass !—and oh, look there,
    What lovely ormolu !"

ALONE!

"The world belongs to cold hearts."—MACHIAVEL.

A THOUSAND millions walk the Earth
  Whom Time and Death control :
Alone ! and lonely from our birth,
  Each one a Separate Soul !

Yet the Great God who made all things,
  And " good " He saw they were,
Gave not to Man a Seraph's wings
  To quit this lower sphere !

(Though sheathèd plumes the spirit hath,
  In Life but half unfurl'd,
To float him o'er its burning path,
  In Thought's aërial world.)

Not wings to bear us far away,
  God gives his creatures here,
But tendrils of the heart which may
  Infold each blessing near.

Affections—sympathies divine—
   High aspirations wake ;
Each seeking with its like to twine,
   And joy to give and take.

These are His gifts, that strongest glow
   In Genius' burning breast,
Which can but half its radiance show,
   Soul-lit at His behest !

Alone !—through Childhood's lagging hours,
   Which creep until our prime,—
Heart-longing, like the folded flowers,
   To reach a gladder time.

Alone !—for even then begin
   The discipline and wrong,
Which crush the nobler soul within,
   And make it of the throng :

Even in just proportion due
   As the young heart is warm
To mould to loftier things and true,
   It takes the shape of harm.

Torn are the tendrils soft and strong,
   That may not cling aright ;
Yet how instinctively, for long,
   They struggled towards the light !

Alone ! We never know how much,
  Till we that trial dare,
When Care, who heaps with stealthy touch,
  Bids us our burthen bear,—

A fardel made of many things,
  Of sorrows unforeseen,
And hopes whose knell keen Memory rings
  To show—what might have been !

Life's errors wreck the little store
  Of Time which moulds our fate :
And seldom beacons shine before,
  But mock us when too late.

Alone—Alone !—each highest thought,
  The one least understood ;
Till oh, in Death—Life's battle fought,
  We are Alone with GOD !

THE PASSING GUEST.

'Tis pleasant in the summer time a Passing Guest to be,
And share 'mong dearly cherish'd friends their hospi-
    tality.
Yet strangely thrills the human heart, that, wheresoe'er
    we roam,
We kiss the chain whose farthest links are twined around
    our home.
And this, methinks, is something like the way it comes
    about,
Though kind attentions but increase, without one thank-
    less doubt ;
Nay, better far one little week among all household ties,
Can make us know and love a friend, than years' for-
    malities.

We've been the pretty rides and walks—a day's excur-
    sion too—
A pic-nic where the rising hills command so fine a view :
" You mark the distant spire that peeps above that mass
    . of green,
A little to the left, and there the ocean may be seen ;

That line of light—yon drooping cloud—just now is in
    the way."
It might be so, and this I know, we had a merry day.

New friends are made, and visits paid of country eti-
    quette,
And of the little children all I 've my peculiar pet.
The eldest son, a noble boy, confides to me the thought,
The hope that soon for him will be a gun and pony
    bought ;
He hints at glorious days to come, when school no more
    shall shackle,
And then explains the mysteries of his new fishing tackle.
His sister dear, 'tis very clear, dreams in her heart so
    still,
" How very fine to be grown up, and do just what one
    will ! "

Ah! foolish girl, strive not to shake the steady glass of
    Time,
For woman's heart and woman's care ring oft a mourn-
    ful chime.
The world hath harsher fetters far to thwart the rebel
    will
Than thou canst image, girt but by the bonds that guard
    from ill ;
Woven by love, enwreath'd with flowers, so lightly do
    they press,
It were a blessed boon to know for aye such happiness !

So weeks pass on with rapid flight, for they are gaily
    pass'd,
And yet upon our distant home some anxious thoughts
    are cast ;
A letter comes—or, it may be, the want of one has power
To make us fix, 'gainst wishes kind, the parting day and
    hour.

The wind has whistled all the night, in threatening
    accents loud,
But now the sun is struggling with a canopy of cloud ;
And through the trees the autumn breeze declares the
    day will be
Not cold nor warm, but just the one we most desired to
    see.
The house is in unusual stir, and boxes crowd the hall,
And something over which, by chance, a travelling cloak
    doth fall ;
One corner peeps of wicker-work, and now I know the
    rest,
For goodly things are often found within a *hamper*
    press'd.

I thought I miss'd the snow-white goose and chickens ;
    and "the birds"
Were what they meant last night, though I but half
    made out the words.
Although I wept, I do not think 'twas for their hapless
    fate,
Though cut off in their very prime, nice appetites to sate :

How strange the chord ; how slight the touch will waken
    smile or tear !
For very unromantic things oft marks of kindness bear.

But few our words ; for tongues that are like streams
    unbound from frost,
At meeting, are the very ones that parting fetters most.
" Put to the horses ; we can do the distance in an hour
Unto 'the Station,' after which we care not for a shower."
The house-dog wags his bushy tail in token of delight,
(" Is it at last you know me, sir, or think to go is
    right ? ")

The Station gained—we pique ourselves on punctuality,
And so have leisure here to say our very last " good
    bye ; "
To give the tearful kiss, and press the hand with cordial
    grasp,
And own how much we'll try next year the very same to
    clasp.
Oh ! blessings on the power that doth, or fair or foul the
    weather,
" Annihilating time and space," bring loving hearts to-
    gether !

And Home is reached with all its joy ; the tongue *is*
    loosened now,
A very cataract of words in rushing stream doth flow.
Our dog not only wags his tail, but to my shoulder leaps,
And shawls and bonnet fall about in most disordered
    heaps.

Though tired, we look in every nook ; I 'm sure I can't
    tell why,
Since walls and floors I never heard were very apt to fly.

Once more, though not till late, my couch I press with
    wearied frame,
And when I wake, a moment pause, to ask how *there* I
    came ?
For dreams have been of those dear friends whom now
    but dreams can bring,
The children's prattle, Lion's bark, or some familiar
    thing ;
The chestnut trees beneath whose shade the spell of
    silence reign'd,
That spirit food which never yet was in the city gain'd ;
All seem'd to haunt my slumbers deep, and soothe a
    dreamer's ear,
Home lured me back—but still I 'm glad they've ask'd
    me for next year !

October, 1842.

LINES

BRIGHT are the chronicles that Memory tɪue
Imprints in golden type ; which can renew
—Whene'er in thoughtful mood we do unroll
Her chequer'd, and most strangely crowded scroll
Reflected glory ! 'Twas the sunlight hour
When my soul basked beneath the spell, and power,
And presence of Thy marvellous creations,
Till saturate by exquisite sensations
Reeled the full heart with its intense delight.
But Memory sheds, like planets in the night,
A borrowed lustre on that inner world
Where the mind's richest treasures are unfurl'd.
I feel it was a privilege most rare
    To revel in the hallowed atmosphere,
Made by thy genius more than common air :
    For thy great soul hath from a loftier sphere
Wrested high things of majesty and grace,
    Then 'prisoning them in senseless clay or stone,
Thou dost vouchsafe that meaner minds may trace
    The lightning thoughts which thou, oh LOUGH ! hast
        known !

Among the Brotherhood of Bards that chose
Pen—chisel—pencil, thou art one of those
Who sway mankind—a bright link in the chain
Of those immortal minds, which in the train
Of their great doings raise the human race,
And are, in their high rightful " pride of place,"
More truly rulers of the world than they
Who bear the crown, and regal sceptre sway.
What is the power of life and death Kings know ?
The spirit-half of man to Mind doth bow.
Oh ! are not they a great and glorious Band,
   As, stretching o'er the old earth's bygone ages,
To fancy's eye they linkèd hand in hand,
   More great than Atlas on the Heathen pages,
Uphold the mighty fabric of the soul,
O'er which Oblivion's waters shall not roll.
Thou hast communed with their spirits pure,
   Already thou art brother of the band,
And in the forms that shall for aye endure
   Thou hast proclaimed thy mission ;—for *they* stand
The deathless records of that well-earned fame
Which doth love, reverence, admiration, claim.
Oh ! that the princely twain (thy teachers both)
   Shakspere and Milton, in some magic glass
Had viewed the subtle and most wondrous growth
   Of their rich legacies, which thou dost pass
By the Promethean, kindred, spark of mind
Into the Marble where they are entwined.
Not thine the tinsel trappings of the stage :
Thou know'st a purer mine—the Poet's Page.

Thy speech I 'll ne'er forget—a sculptor's " duty "
To shrine in more than words *his* Dreams of Beauty.
But turn we from poor mad Ophelia, or
The subtle fiend Iago—conqueror
(As the snake conquers by a poison wound)
   Of the brave Moor of Venice and his bride.
We 'll break the potent spell *this* flings around,
   And quit the wonders gathered at its side,
And Venus stealing with a kiss away,
   A dangerous weapon from her wayward son,
And him the fisher boy that 'neath the ray
   Of loved Italia's sun, ere day be done
Repairs the needful fabric ;—and the maid,
The Roman Girl with heavy raven braid—
Whose was the blood that tinged her rounded cheek ?
Who—who—her sires ?—can nought but echo speak
To tell if she be of Patrician race,
   If her sires walked the Cæsars' marble halls,
Or wore the toga in the senate place ?
   But for heart-homage there are other calls—
The Prince of Darkness, yea, a PRINCE indeed,
Sits Throned !—as if the better thence to read
And plan the fortunes of a falling world.
'Tis he from Heaven's empyreal arch was hurl'd,
The potentate to whom the choice was given,
" To rule a king in Hell or serve in Heaven !"
The Majesty of Ill !   We see revealed
The lip of scorn, the hate but half-concealed,
The anguish that the eye-balls cannot hide,
Despair, and yet indomitable Pride.

The clenchèd hand proclaims the will to dare,
The firm-set foot the fortitude to bear.
We understand 'twas no ignoble Foe
That warr'd with Man, and work'd his greatest woe !
The breath comes thick—once more we look around,
And feel indeed we tread on hallowed ground,
Made sacred by the high mysterious spell
That only Genius knows to weave so well !
We turn to leave the feast of intellect,
   That the rapt soul with eager gaze drinks in—
Expression fails—no words I can select
   Convey th' emotions that are felt within ;
And yet it is a luxury—how great !
The power, and privilege, to venerate !

June, 1842.

THE MANIAC.

OH, wherefore do they make me bear this heavy Iron
    Crown ?
I cannot move it, though it bows my very spirit down.
What though I had not beauty's gift,—was wilful,
    strange and wild,
'Twas hard to feel that no one prized the dull, unlovely
    child !
My mother pass'd her fingers through my brother's
    golden hair ;
She us'd to kiss *his* smooth round cheek, for he was
    wondrous fair.

Yes, I was very desolate ; and Envy then, I know,
First tightly bound a silken thread across my Baby brów ;
It hardened to a band of steel, in Youth's gay sunny
    spring ;
But youth was never gay to me—a doomed and blighted
    thing.
Or could it be, I ne'er was young—that grief's maturing
    hand
Led me some other road to age than through that
    flowery land ?

Yes, it was thus ; not ever mine, aught that our youth
    should claim ;
Companionship or bright-eyed hope, I only knew by
    name ;
And love I sought, but never found a shrine whereon to
    lay
The deep and treasured thoughts that cast o'er life one
    sparkling ray ;
Existence was a dreary waste ; but this indeed was
    given—
To have a bright and glorious dream, that will be True
    in Heaven !

One eve I wandered to a rock which overhangs the sea,
And stands unshaken by the storm—the dearest spot to
    me ;
The sea-birds fled (all had their nests), for near the
    tempest's birth ;
Each wild wave kiss'd a lowering cloud, and all was
    noisy mirth.
I strove to mingle in the flood, but demons held me
    down,
And then with regal pomp They placed this Heavy Iron
    Crown !

My throne an ebon cloud they made—I 'd vassal subjects
    too,
The waves bowed in obeisance, and passed beneath my
    view ;

THE MANIAC.

And still uprose the hurricane, and heaved each sno⸱
  crest ;
I thought the storm almost as wild as that within ɪ
  breast !
And now It burns into my brain, and bows my spi
  down :
Oh, Death will surely take away this Heavy Iron Crow⸱

1838.

JOSEPHINE.

A DRAMATIC SKETCH.

——◆——

SCENE.—*A Dressing-Room.*

Ex-Empress JOSEPHINE *and* ATTENDANT.

JOSEPHINE.

Why dost thou linger, girl ?

ATTENDANT.

              But to consult
What robes my Mistress chooses for to-day.

JOSEPHINE.

Ah, true ; they should be costly !—'broidery
And gold ;—velvet from Genoa's peerless loom,
And jewels rare.—Wilt thou not deck me so ?
For is not this a gala day for France,
Where all is joy and revelry ?   Thou hast
No need to tremble, nor thy cheek to pale,
Nor eyes to fill with tears.—Why dost thou weep,
For I cannot ?

ATTENDANT.

           My own dear Mistress !

JOSEPHINE.
Say,
Tell me in truth what day this is ?—My dreams
Are strange,—so very strange ;—is it a dream ?
Or is this day the one, which gives to—to—

ATTENDANT.
To France another Empress !

JOSEPHINE.
Unto *him*
Another Wife! Yes, yes, it is all true ;
Oh God ! his voice is ringing in my ears :
I cannot quell the sound.

ATTENDANT.
Pray, pray be calm.

JOSEPHINE.
And now he whispers to her soft and low :
I see him bend,—he stoops to clasp her hand.
Oh, blindness—deafness—were rich blessings,—so
They shut out Memory too ! Hark, hark ! they cry,
The people cry—" Long live Marie Louise ! "

ATTENDANT.
'Tis fancy, dearest lady.

JOSEPHINE.
May she prove
A blessing unto France and unto him !

K

ATTENDANT.

Whether her days pass on in steady pomp ;
The river of her bright career uncheck'd
By ills, that Fortune flings across the path,
E'en of her favourites ; or the storms which come
Ruffling the stream of life, and casting up
The soul's rich treasures, which perchance had else
Lain all unheeded 'neath the calm deep tide.
(Alas ! that stormy trials e'er should throw
Unto life's surface only common earth.)
Whether in characters of light her name
Be writ, or leave faint trace behind, still thine,
Oh Josephine, will ever on the page
Of the historian shine, like a bright gem
Amid the tinsel glare, that doth indeed
Too oft make up the show of human glory.
France will remember thine, the gentle voice,
To sue for mercy, aye, and win it from
Thy conquering lord, e'en in his fiercest mood ;
And at the last——

JOSEPHINE.
                        What then ?

ATTENDANT.
                  Thou didst give up
The deep, and tried, and treasured love of years,
And power, high station,—all, because they said
'Twas for the weal of France.   Oh, never doubt
That thou art dearly loved.

JOSEPHINE.
To think so is
Most sweet.—But leave me now a little while.
And yet I pray thee first to fling aside
That heavy curtain :—let the bright sun's rays,
Whose glaring lustre seems to mock, not cheer,
The joyless, breaking heart,—let them stream forth
Upon the spot where yonder mirror leans.
                                        [*Exit* ATTENDANT
(After a pause.)
They say that She is passing fair ;—with form
And face, to win the homage Beauty claims ;
A girlish thing, who, from her years, might be
His daughter.   But the youthful heart that should .
Have mated with her early pledge was mine,
In its first flush of ardent passion ; when
Within his soul Ambition was a flame
To light, even to purify—not burn.
But now its raging heat has withered up
All gentler feelings.   From his fellow-men
Far raised, and set apart,—the wildest dream
Of his hot youth seems, in its memory,
A faint imperfect shadow.   Yet how sweet
It was with mingled minds to interchange,
Or share those glorious visions, which, alas !
Though pictured then by Hope's bright pencil, dipp'd
In rainbow hues, reach'd and o'erleap'd, seemed mean .
And worthless.   But *She* cannot know all this.
The Royal Maiden born, nurtured in pomp
And pride, can never tell what 'twas to build
                        K 2

A Throne from the disjointed fragments which
An earthquake had o'erwhelmed.   And she, perchance,
Accustomed to the giddy height, may feel
No trembling lest the stormy elements
But slumber in their strength.   She cannot read
The language of His eye, or brow,—the thought
The *fear* that never yet found utterance
In words !   Be still, my jealous heart, be still ;
'Tis true the Emperor loves his bride,—he loves
As in a dozen years a man may love
A dozen different women ; but he loves
Her not as Josephine was loved, in those
Delicious days, before the vulture, blind
And ravenous Ambition, gnawed his heart
Away.

    And now, my mirror,—on thy clear
And polished surface I can trace my form
The same as yesterday, and that again
Seemed like its predecessor ;—and again
Through days, and weeks, and months, and years the
  same,
Even thy surface (Truth's own emblem) failed
To warn me of the subtle work of that
Arch-spoiler Time, who doth, with steady hand
And sure, the chisel wield from day to day ;—.
At first to model to perfection,—then
Destroy.   I marvel if mine eye be still
As bright as when he praised its lustre,—or
These hands as soft as when they clasp'd his own,—
Or is my form the same his arms entwined ?

I cannot tell ; the image of one's self
Is the sole record memory imprints
In ever-shifting sand.

                  And we shall meet
With Friendship's even pulse ;—our converse light
And careless !   But I 'll don the armour proof—
A woman's pride :—and none, not He, shall tell
That her loved France, even the Universe,
Is to poor Josephine a dreary waste,
In which the boon she asks is but a Grave !

    1840.

SONNET.

Another Noon—and still the Sun rides high,
  Without the shadow of a gathering cloud ;
  The parch'd blade withers on the earth ; a crowd
Of pale young flowers stoop down their heads to die,
And lordly trees look up despairingly !
  The streams have shrunk, like miser's store whose heirs
  Awhile have revelled on their parted shares ;
And Nature faints beneath the fervid sky.
So blighting hours pass on, till Evening comes,
  When lo ! with Night ascending from the east,
See dark-fringed messengers, to glad the homes
  Of prince and peasant ! Oh, of them the least
Is sign and banner of a conquering train,
For thirsty Earth drinks in the blessèd Rain !

    July, 1844.

THE DEATH OF LEONARDO DA VINCI.

SUGGESTED BY THE FINE ENGRAVING OF MR. FISK'S EXQUISITE
PICTURE REPRESENTING LEONARDO DA VINCI DYING IN THE
ARMS OF FRANCIS THE FIRST.

Oh, mighty is the Painter's art,
   For it alone can reach
The things and thoughts that lie too deep
   For Poet's power of speech !
Yet fitfully the numbers come
   When Painted Poems glow,
As if our own rich northern tongue
   Its sympathy would show ;
And struggle e'en to wake a tone,
   How poor soe'er may be
The lyre which comes the first to hand,
   To serve its minstrelsy !

Within yon sumptuous chamber now,
   Who sees a King is there ?—
A crownèd King of princely heart,
   And ever regal air.

The homage which he yields, 'tis true,
   Gives back a radiant fame,
That wins a deeper reverence far
   Than any other claim ;
But *here* are Kings more great than he !
   King Death asserts his right,
Whose solemn Presence wrestles now
   With Life's expiring light !

Not terror, but a conscious awe
   Shines through the dying face
On which the gaze of Francis rests,
   As he each line would trace.
Oh Life and Death, a fearful sight
   To watch the conflict dread,
Which is the prelude to the hour
   When vanquished hope has fled !

But greater than an earthly King,
   And greater than King Death,
The Majesty of Genius is,
   Surviving parted breath ;
Dwelling a Spirit on the earth,
   Though dust to dust returns ;
For such as He have left a light
   Which still serenely burns !

I marvel not no terrors rest
   Upon Da Vinci's brow ;
His works proclaim his soul had known
   But holy thoughts below.

I marvel not his head should lean
    Upon a monarch's breast ;
That monarch knew that Genius' self
    Was worthy holiest rest.

But nobler than of old is *now*
    The part that Genius fills ;
It teaches thousands for but one,
    And all its lore instils ;
Makes light in myriad darkened minds,
    And through the 'graver's art
Is multiplied yet hundred-fold,
    And plays the Teacher's part !

THE EARTH.

—•—

" And God saw that it was good."

THE Earth ! Methinks the thoughtless are too prone
   To rail against this fruitful flowering earth ;
" HE saw that it was good," when from His throne
   His will decreed this wondrous planet's birth !
Perchance from crumbling dust, uprose the hills,
   But crumbling dust Created must have been ;
And rushing torrents, with soft murmuring rills,
   Leap'd from their heights, or lav'd the meadows green !
Then gathering ocean foam'd, and girt the world
Like a full mantle round its vastness furl'd ;
And Nature's varied music, far and near,
First woke the slumbering echoes deep and clear ;
And then was by the " wandering wind " begun,
The pilgrimage that is not yet outrun.

Surely with joy surcharged, stood forth the Earth
Matured—a giant at its glorious birth !
" God saw that all was good," and 'tis His will
Which doth permit that ill should chequer still
His bright creation.   And shall feeble man
Presume His wise and wondrous scheme to scan ?

The Earth is His, 'twas He the wonder made,
And pois'd it in unfathomable space :
Do *they* not doubt His wisdom, who array'd
In frowns, lament their present dwelling-place ?
The Earth is very fair to human eyes—
Though Error veils the mortal paradise
With a dark cloud, which yet we pierce e'en here,
For Hope and Faith reveal the holier sphere !

And there are lesser ladders we may link
Together, till they touch almost the brink
Of that deep chasm, which the human mind
In life must not o'erleap ; but sweet we find
The upward path—more sure each airy rail
That doth for such high purposes avail.
Do we not climb such ladders when we ope
The book of marvellous Science, or give scope
To the ingushings of true Poesy,
Whose fountain flows o'er all created things,
And is a Baptism of Divinity,
Still ever rising from exhaustless springs !
And music is a link whose strange control
Laps in elysium the human soul :
But most the power of contemplation given,
Is surely foretaste of a future heaven !
Unto the thoughtful mind Life is one prayer,
And earth's pure pleasures Adoration there !

1842.

THE QUEEN OF SPRING.

HAIL to the Queen!—the Queen of Spring!
She hath journey'd here on the zephyr's wing ;
Like a young coquette, she hath linger'd a while,
That we may rejoice in her song and smile !
But we know she has come, for her perfumed breath
Hath awaken'd the earth from its fooming death,
She has spoken the word, and the messenger breeze
Hath whisper'd her will to the shivering trees ;
Their pale green leaves they have all unfurl'd,
And the Spirit of Youth is abroad in the world !

Hail to the Queen!—the Queen of Spring !
That has journey'd here on the zephyr's wing.
Let us twine her a wreath from the sunny bowers
Of the violet blue and young wild flowers,
And the valley's lily that grows beside,
And always looks like the violet's bride.
But see!—here are roses as white as snow,
They are fitting to bind on her fair young brow ;
And their deep-glowing sisters, whose hue first begun
From a blush at the praises their loveliness won ;
While the sun with warm kisses, in whispers the air,
Still tell the same story, and hold the Blush there !

But the roses are come !—She must hasten away,
Or the Southern World will mourn for her stay !
On the zephyr's wing she is sailing now—
She has many a league to cross, ye know.
For her car she hath taken a warm bright beam,
And is fading away like a happy dream.
The sun rides high in the heavens again,
The flowers have burst from their emerald chain ;
So their beautiful ruler, the Queen of Spring,
Her sceptre has pass'd to the Summer King !

1838.

WHAT DOST THOU WHISPER,
MURMURING SHELL?

WHAT dost thou whisper, murmuring Shell?
  Child of the fathomless dark sea.
Thou canst great Ocean's secrets tell ;
  Oh, then, proclaim thy lore to me !
Teach me the language of thy tone.
  What would thy cold, still lips reveal ?
All the dread mysteries thou hast known,
  Oh, not for ever thus conceal !
What dost thou whisper, murmuring Shell?
Wouldst thou dread Ocean's secrets tell ?

Bear'st thou unto some heart bereaved
  A message that, from parting breath,
Thy apt and ready form received,
  Ere Beauty found her bridegroom— Death ?
Or didst thou leave the wide domain,
  And thy bright home in coral cave,
To echo Man's shrill cry of pain,
  Ere life was vanquish'd by the wave ?
What dost thou whisper, murmuring Shell?
Wouldst thou dark Ocean's secrets tell ?

A SONG FOR SEPTEMBER.

LONDON 's empty !   Only in it
  Something near two million souls ;
Some in cellars, some in garrets,
  Some the work-house law controls !
Crime, barefaced, in prisons wasting
  (Also hid on beds of down,
After days of pleasure tasting,
  Either in or out of town).

London 's empty !   Only in it
  Merchants' fructifying store ;
And misers' dull " enchanted " treasure,
  Which the spider watches o'er.
Hark ! the wail of sorrow sighing,
  Tears are shedding every minute ;
Every day a hundred dying,
  Though the town has " nothing " in it !

Joy and grief—all human passions—
  Love and anger, peace and strife :
On what inner worlds of feeling
  Turn the outer wheels of Life,
Though ITS mighty heart is beating
  With a dull lethargic flow,
After Senators' grave meeting,
  After Fashion's fever glow !

LINES ON A PORTRAIT.

Rosy lips and gentle eyes,
Tresses catching many dyes,
 Whene'er the sunbeams find thee ;
Grace and beauty are thine own,
Weaving thee a fairy zone,
 As if to guard and bind thee.

Yet a dearer wealth thou hast,
Which must be but of the Past,
 When years have flitted o'er thee ;
That morn which breaks on childhood's sleep,—
That heritage we may not keep—
 Bright YOUTH is all before thee !

When mere existence is a sense,
So tuned by Hope to Joy intense,
 E'en sorrow 's half a pleasure ;
When nestle near the heart bright things,
Like radiant birds, whose folded wings
 Half hide their gorgeous treasure.

The ruffling of their wings for flight
Just shows us how exceeding bright
    Youth's radiant guests have been ;
But 'tis when their sweet stay is sped,
And pinions wide are all outspread,
    That every hue is seen.

Fair Girl ! in Life's yet early spring
May Youth its ample treasures bring,
    Its world whose light is Truth ;
And know that as thou usest them
Shall shine through Life that mirror gem,
    The Memory of Youth !

THE CRY OF THE FELON.

SUGGESTED BY MR. DICKENS'S LETTER ON THE "RAGGED SCHOOLS," IN "THE DAILY NEWS" OF FEB. 4, 1846.

YES ! shackle my limbs, and bind me fast,
   Through the hooting crowd to press,
Away to the Judgment Hall ; at last
   The Doom of my Life I guess.
Think not the spasm that shoots through my frame
   Is the quiver of wounded pride ;
What hath the Felon to do with shame,
   Or the pangs unto shame allied !

Ye are ranged as Foes—and my heart *will* swell
   With hate and a dull despair ;
Though your laws compel that the Lie I tell
   With a calm and truthful air.
Oh, were it not brave if I cheated you,
   Ye Judges sage and cold !
My thin blood warms at the thought anew,
   And the Lie grows strong and bold.

L

Grave Judges, 'tis *I* who have wrongs to revenge,
  More than You in your ermined state ;
And the God who through Us doth the wrong avenge,
  Worketh out a Nation's fate.
How dared you leave me to fester my soul
  Through Misery's keen temptations—
Where Infamy's gulfing waters roll,
  And Example finds persuasions ?

My world was a night—where Ignorance lay
  Like a pall o'er my trampled heart ;
I never knew childhood's careless day,
  Nor aught that could joy impart.
Tell me not Power cannot touch this Wrong—
  It hath skill to bring Me here ;
It hath gold to fee the slippery tongue
  Of my foe, the pleader there.

It hath strength to mould that marvel great—
  An army of willing men ;
And to rest secure in pride and state,
  Above the vulgar ken.
Surely it were a lighter task
  To scatter a little gold !
Feed us, and Teach us, are all we ask,
  And the Pauper YOUTH to mould !

Ye 've heard of the mansions fair and great
  Which the Rats have undermined ;
We are the Rats of the Social State,
  Which ye seek to trap and bind.

And this, when ye have a Wizard Wand
   (As of old in the fairy tale)
By which ye could change us to a band
   Of servitors true and hale !

Feb. 1846.

SONNET.

"The heart knoweth its own bitterness."

I WILL commune with mine own heart alone,
   So learn to battle with the giant Grief
   That shadows now my soul, and reigns a chief ;
Quenching each spark of joy and hope that shone
Till sick, faint Reason trembles on her throne.
   Oh Heart ! grow greater, bring me thus relief,
   Make room for chaos and a new belief !
So—so—it may be borne. All but the tone
Of the word-arrows friendly tongues would fling,
   Calling them sweet advice ! I do beseech
Believe me—and not meaner counsel bring
   Than the great truths which greatest poets teach ;
Great Grief is all too Great and True a thing
   For the world's narrow policy to reach !

FLING BACK THE SCORN!

HOMAGE TO THE MARTYRS OF THE 62ND REGIMENT, ENGAGED AT FEROZESHAH.

" The troops were exposed to tremendous fires from batteries, which altogether numbered twenty large battering guns, distributed in different parts of the entrenched works, and forty-two guns of smaller calibre. When they came within range of this iron storm, against which they were moving with the greatest firmness, at one particular time, within ten minutes, seventeen of the twenty-one officers of the 62nd, twelve sergeants, and one half of the men were struck down. The commanding officer was one of the number * * * *. The energies of the men must have been weakened by exposure to the sun and want of water * * * * The regiment had but four hundred men left and four officers * * * *. The previous conduct of this regiment, and the extent to which they suffered, from the tremendous and crushing fire to which they were exposed, ought to obliterate for ever the effect of a temporary panic."—*Speech of Sir Howard Douglas.*

FLING back the Scorn in the Scorner's teeth,
    Ye remnant brave but stricken ;
For ye have looked i' the face of Death,
    And seen his Terrors thicken.

Fling back the Scorn—but do not stoop
    To humble exculpation,
Nor ask compassion for the troop
    Who merit admiration !

Be sure the GOD whose every law
  To love and joy doth tend,
Who in the Past the Future saw,
  This Satan's game will end.

And—for HE works with human means—
  Let us the task begin,
To strip the mask from " Glory's " scenes,
  And view the Truth within !

Let Scorners borrow Fancy's aid,
  Though weak her pencil be,
And faint the pictures thus portrayed
  Beside reality.

Yet 'tis enough : ye see a band—
  Eight hundred fellow-men—
All exiles from the native land
  How few shall see again !

Foot-sore with weary, weary march,
  Athirst ! No water nigh ;
No food ; and night—yet Heaven's arch
  Their only canopy !

And think the inner life that dwells
  In every human breast :
Its love, or hope, or fear that swells
  To be a ruling guest !

Yet faint, exhausted, on they lead,
   To meet the "iron shower,"
Nor quailed till half their numbers dead
   Beneath its murderous power.

Not till their captains fell like reeds,
   Sway'd by the tempest's breath—
More wise to live for future deeds
   Than rush on CERTAIN Death !

God ! what a scene for Angels' eyes
   A field of battle is !
God ! what a scene for star-lit skies
   Was horror like to this !

Rivers of blood the arid sand
   Suck'd in like crimson rain ;
While quivering flesh on either hand
   Bestrew'd the accursèd plain :

Dissevered limbs, and trampled clay,
   In strange and ghastly heaps,
Proclaim the horrors of the day
   Where Death his harvest reaps :

Features distorted, and on some
   Unutterable sadness ;
Others to deeper depths had come—
   The hell of Torture's madness !

From parchèd throats the wail is heard
   Of " Water—water send ! "
Or " Oh, dear comrade, hear a word—
   Your sword this anguish end ! "

Fling back the Scorn ! again I say,
   Ye were the bravest brave ;
And sad Misfortune's sombre ray
   Should hallow every grave.

Fling back the Scorn ! Survivors few,
   Yours is the Martyr's crown,
Seen by the sunlight of the True,
   In glory all your own.

Oh, what a poor and fading wreath
   Success alone can twine !
The Martyr's Life, or Martyr's Death
   Weaves one far more divine !

March 3rd, 1846.

THE DOOMED.

SUGGESTED BY HEARING THE NARRATIVE OF A VOYAGE TO MADEIRA.

ONWARD she sailed ;—with her most precious freight—
Bound for the sunny isle, where grow the vine
And myrtle.   Ev'ry breeze that lightly stirred
The sails, whispered with Hope's melodious voice
Unto *The Doomed*, the tale that they were saved !
For there were three of these, on whose fair brows
Had dread Consumption fixed his withering seal,
Choosing his victims, like a vampire fiend,
Among the young and beautiful !

     The first
Of them, a friendless orphan girl, had pass'd
Into the bloom that eighteen summers bring ;
Yet scarce a creature of the earth she seemed.
There are who say, the dying strange things see,
And I have sometimes thought she must have held
Communion with the unseen world, she was
So spiritualized.   She had not known
A joy, or sorrow ; there was not a link
To bind her soul to earth ;—and a pure faith

THE DOOMED.

No cloud had ever dimm'd, gave her e'en now
To taste of Heaven.   This the first that died :
Her sepulchre the ocean deep and blue ;
And tempest dread, for her sad requiem !

The second was a girl of twenty.   Rich
And gifted, loving and beloved.   One night,
One glorious night,—when glitt'ring o'er the wave
Danced the phosphoric light, as if to mock
The thousand eyes that beamed so bright in Heaven,—
Half angry, that they tried to thwart her will,
She still with playful pettishness besought
That she might view the scene so many praised ·
Saying, as they threw a mantle o'er her,
" There 's not a breeze to move a loosened curl."
And then she gazed upon the calm blue sky,
And near to her was he whom she adored,
His arm wound gently round her ; yet awhile
They both were silent.   She was first to speak.
" I love the stars—and love therein to read
The stories which are writ, it seems on leaves
Of gold ; as if the ancient sages thought
To link for ever to the Universe
The mem'ry of their heroes.   Glorious orbs !
Ye tell me only of the past and future.
A myst'ry and a poetry ye have
Which science cannot dull ; and ever thus
On such a night will Fancy slip the rein
Stern Reason holds and airy fabrics build.
But I am dying,   Dearest, you will watch

The stars alone ! ''   Her head then softly lean'd
Upon his shoulder, but her bright eyes gazed
Yet on the spangled heavens : whilst he breathed
The words of confidence, by Hope beguiled
So often, that he did in truth believe
Her joyful lesson.   Of the southern clime
He spoke, of Italy, where they would dwell
After a little while.   And then the words,
Th' impassion'd eloquence, the warm, true heart
Will ever teach, burst from his lips : and tears,
But tears that are not born of sorrow, came
Silent and few, over a cheek whose flush
Lent more than mortal beauty to her face.
Softly she murmur'd, " In an hour like this
'Twere not so hard to die ;—it has been mine
To taste the brightest drop life's chalice holds :
Why should I sigh to drink its dregs, and yet ''——

A gifted son of genius was the third,
Though manhood's early dawn was scarcely pass'd ;
The thirst, the deep unquenching thirst for fame
Was his ; the thought that he should leave his name
" Familiar in men's mouths as household words,"
Sustained him now ; the wreath but nobly won,
He little cared that it might only deck
An early grave.   With burning cheek, and eyes
That flashed, his glowing pages he would read
Unto the maiden and her lover ;—theirs
That spark which, genius though it may not be,
Perchance of something kindred is, the power

To know and taste the banquet that it spreads!
Are not the praise and gratitude of such
The poet's guerdon?   In his gayer hours,
A song of chivalry or lady's love
He 'd weave into "immortal verse;" and she
Would wed it unto harmony of sound,
And make the air melodious with her voice:
And for awhile they both forgot that Death
Relentless stalked between them, with his dart
Already poised!

    And these two reached the isle.
The youth sank first—he had a poet's grave,
For Heaven's vault was a more fitting dome
Than are the temples where they bury princes.
And for the beautiful and loved! she drooped
And died, just like the last flower autumn spares,
That withers leaf by leaf.   But she was noble
So her they carried to her father-land,
And in the marble tomb she moulders now
Beside her lordly line!

 1838.

ON THE CLOSE OF THE YEAR.

No wonder poets choose thee for their theme,
Great Time ! And if the lay be weak, 'twould seem
Even from thy sublimity, to gain
Both power and glory,—borrowed not in vain ;
For peerless attar, 'prisoned in dull clay,
Doth make the poor earth rich, though pass'd away,
Leaving a legacy of wealth behind.
'Tis thus we seek embodiment to find
Of those high thoughts, which, like an essence rare,
Men fain would bind and keep ; for this they share
The subtle power or spirit with some thing
Of meaner quality, and strive to bring,
And hold, within their reach that spirit-power
Impalpable as fragrance from a flower.
So poets strive to summon at their call
Th' embalming words, which, if they come at all,
The best and brightest are but earthy things,
    Dimming the radiance they should enshrine,
Too weak to follow Thought's aspiring wings,
    Or pierce the depths of its unfathom'd mine !

Thou of the iron rule, great Time !—the thought
    Of thee is all so vast, we cannot hope
    To find for it a prison in the scope

Of narrow words ;—enough if there be caught
Some feeble sparks, in kindred minds to light
A flame, which there may grow more clear and bright.

They fashion thee, old Time, with wings outspread ;
   Yet I could think that sometimes they are furl'd,
When thou dost move with halt and lagging tread,
   Casting a shadow on that inner world
The mind itself creates.   Lovers do count
   The shadow'd days of absence, dark indeed
To the true heart, which eagerly would mount
   The car of Phœbus, that each lazy steed
Might mend its pace, and gallop to the goal
Which seems so sadly distant to his soul.
Neither, methinks, dost thou too swiftly roll
For them Ambition lures !   Expectant train,
Who strut along beneath their galling chain
Proudly, because 'tis gilt ; looking in vain
To meteor fires, which mock their ardent chase,
Neglecting flowers each crushes in the race.

And there are others, too, who sometimes chide
   The tardy pace of Time.   In these there meet
Bright intellect and heart ; with the high tide
   Of keen sensations—waters pure and sweet
To mirror fleeting joys ; but dark and deep
Their under currents, where ingulfed there sleep
The wrecks of precious things.   And such do long
And yearn for years to swiftly pass along
Till " Times " shall be less " out of joint " with all

Those revelations of a loftier state.
They see the twilight, and they feel the pall
   Which covers this fair laughing Earth—though late—
Will be by Time removed—and would not stay
His rapid onward flight.   Let him away !

What does Time rob us of ?—our Youth !—That wealth
   Which we look back on through the golden gate
   That ne'er shall ope again.   With heart elate,
Youth is but little prized, until by stealth
We feel it shrinking, like a hoarded store,
   On which th' inheritor draws heavy drafts.
   So they were just, methinks no bitter shafts
Are left to rankle when our youth is o'er !
Who would give back the fruits of riper years
   For the mere blossoms, or the produce crude
Of the May-days of life—their Hopes and Fears ?
   Both hollow cheats, which most in youth intrude
To misdirect our steps :—the world we find,
Its joys and dangers, different to the mind,
(Greater or less, but still of different hue,)
From the false scenes they conjured to our view !

But myriad are the clinging memories,
Which unto earth's "tired denizens" must rise
Whene'er the mind, as now, just stays to mark
The pauseless tread of Time !—Into thy dark
And measureless abyss, Eternity,
A few more sands are dropt.—Eternity !
That is a thing too vast for human speech,

Which soaring thought itself can never reach !
Enough, created Time sprang from thy womb,
Of which thou art as well the mighty tomb !
Let us not mourn the rapid flight of Time,

   The world grows richer ev'ry hour we live ;
Not in the drossy store of India's clime,

   But in the dearer wealth that mind can give.
Pass o'er us then, old Time, with wings outspread,

   Scatt'ring the blessings which shall still endure,
" Rip'ning and rotting" as our path we tread,

   And healing wounds which only thou canst cure !

Dec. 1041.

SONNET—EVENING.

I LOVE to watch the bright Stars, one by one,
   As, rushing through the veil of early Night,
   By tiny rents, they struggle into light,
Breathless and trembling, when their race is done.
Watch! ye will see each mount its golden throne,
   Pierce, with a stedfast gaze, the ether gray,
   And ye will see outspring each sparkling ray,
Shining as when the world was young they shone.
And Earth looks up with an unwrinkled brow!
   And shall she thus a Hebe-Mother stand
For countless ages still? I only know
   How much I love to watch the quaint-named band
With dim imaginings; for they will look
Upon the wonders of Her Future's sealèd book!

THE END.

LONDON:
BRADBURY AND EVANS, PRINTERS, WHITEFRIARS.

BIBLIOBAZAAR

The essential book market!

Did you know that you can get any of our titles in our trademark **EasyRead**^{TM} print format? **EasyRead**^{TM} provides readers with a larger than average typeface, for a reading experience that's easier on the eyes.

Did you know that we have an ever-growing collection of books in many languages?

Order online:
www.bibliobazaar.com

Or to exclusively browse our **EasyRead**^{TM} collection:
www.bibliogrande.com

At BiblioBazaar, we aim to make knowledge more accessible by making thousands of titles available to you – quickly and affordably.

Contact us:
BiblioBazaar
PO Box 21206
Charleston, SC 29413